"They'll attack you this morning, and they'll come a-booming when they come—skirmishers three deep. You watch! You'll have to fight like the devil to hold out until supports get here."

—A Union general discussing the impending
Confederate attack with a fellow officer

More Landmarks in History

GETTYSBURG

by MacKinlay Kantor

Random House New York

http://www.randomhouse.com/

Library of Congress Cataloging-in-Publication Data
Kantor, MacKinlay. Gettysburg. (Landmark Books)
SUMMARY: Describes the bloodiest engagement of the
Civil War—the Battle of Gettysburg—and its impact on the
people in that part of Pennsylvania.
1. Gettysburg, Battle of, 1863–Juvenile literature.
2. Gettysburg (Pa.)–History–Juvenile literature.
[1. Gettysburg, Battle of, 1863. 2. United States–History–
Civil War, 1861–1865–Campaigns.] I. Title.
E475.53.K3 1987b 973.7`349 87-4576
ISBN: 0-394-89181-3 (trade)

Printed in the United States of America
20 19 18 17 16 15 14 13

CONTENTS

1

JA, THE REBELS EAT BABIES!

Before the battle swept Gettysburg there happened a number of exciting things, and some frightening things and funny things as well. War is not wholly serious; not everything which occurs in battle is tragic. Somehow the sad matters and fearful matters and exciting matters are mingled like clover and weeds in Pennsylvania hay.

There was clover at Gettysburg and wheat, too, gleaming in summer afternoons. There were fruit orchards where fat cherries had already been picked, where later peaches and apples would ripen and grow tender, waiting for days when children would climb on homemade ladders to fill their baskets with good fruit.

At least that is what people of the Gettysburg region and of all Adams County thought would

3

happen, in June of 1863. The soil had always been harvested according to Nature's plan and man's. No one could imagine a future wherein masses of still-green peaches were torn from boughs before the proper season, split and ruined by a billion bits of lead and steel—the terrible sleet of the greatest battle ever fought in America.

Gettysburg was a contented town, long settled, well built with solid houses. Perhaps fifteen hundred people lived there at the time of the Civil War. The town has grown, but even nowadays it could not be called a city.

Gettysburg folks prided themselves on the fact that they had sent noted sons into public life. Thaddeus Stevens was a former resident, a busy statesman whose name was famous. Other young folks of Gettysburg might grow up to be famous, too, for they had every opportunity for a good education. A Lutheran seminary rose in proud brick state on a long ridge west or slightly northwest of the village, and you could see the cupola of that tall building for miles around.

From far down the Emmitsburg Road where Maryland lay a few miles distant, you could see the cupola. You could see it from Round Top, a bulging, tree-covered hill, and from Little Round Top, a shaggy, rocky hill nearby. From all the way up the pleasant farm-clad ridge to the north you could see it too. This elevation was called

Granite Ridge in those days. Now people call it Cemetery Ridge.

You could stand in Ever Green Cemetery, at the end of Granite Ridge—you could stand amid old-fashioned tombstones and look out through bushes where warblers chattered about their summer business, and you could see the eggshell of the seminary cupola, away over beyond the town. If you had been a boy or a girl in the middle of June 1863, it would never have occurred to you that that queer structure above the distant roof could serve as a watchtower for strained and angry soldiers.

Out north of town there was another school, called Penn College or State College; there were schools for children in the village. The townspeople had a fine level of intelligence and lived their lives in decency and pride. So did the well-fed Pennsylvania German farm families who occupied most of the nearby region. They were hardworking people who were interested chiefly in their calves or colts or fattening pigs, and in the best use of their pastures.

The war was far to the south; folks could not believe that a conflict would ever roll through upper Virginia, through low mountains of Maryland, and into their own fair county to disturb them. Most of the healthy young men of the community had already gone to the war, now in its

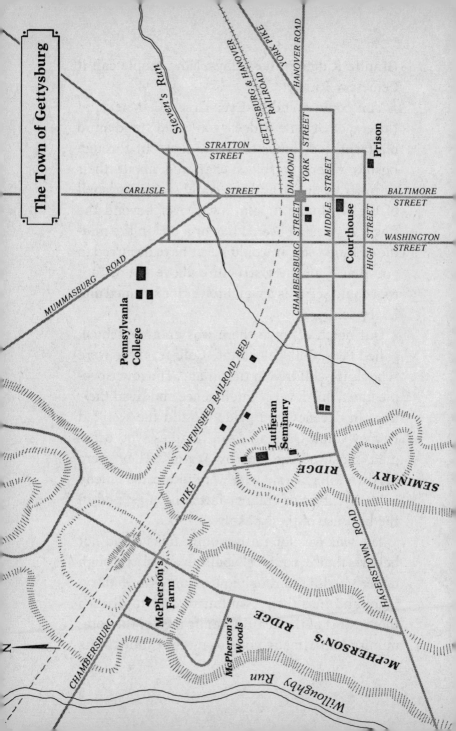

third year. Some had been killed; a few bodies of unfortunate youths who perished had been shipped home. It was strange to look at the fresh-turned earth above their graves after they were put to rest on the cemetery hill.

Sometimes wayward boys had gone up to Ever Green Cemetery—perhaps they sneaked off with an elder brother's rifle or shotgun. There were chipmunks and rabbits to stalk, but the explosion of hunters' weapons was far different from the vast stammer of muskets in a battle, different from the ear-ringing roar of artillery fire. Gettysburg officials did not approve of such antics in a sacred place where their dead lay quiet. A sign had been put up at the gate:

ALL PERSONS FOUND USING FIREARMS IN
THESE GROUNDS WILL BE PROSECUTED WITH
THE UTMOST VIGOR OF THE LAW.

There! said the officials. That should serve as proper warning to anyone who dared think of carrying a weapon into such a place.

Until the last week of June, the youth of Gettysburg had been busy with ordinary chores and play: helping their mothers in the garden, gathering eggs, going on errands to an uncle's house or a grandparent's. In warm, flowery dusk they played I Spy, and Toss the Wicket, and Run, Sheep, Run. . . .

But a strange, dark threat built itself like sudden rain clouds beyond Oak Ridge, where the seminary stood. Danger dwelt where the Chambersburg Pike (some people called it the Cashtown Road) cut across McPherson's Ridge and ambled northwest to the village of Cashtown and the larger town of Chambersburg—a distant place, to be sure. Few of the inhabitants of this small town had ever been so far from home.

A menace was assembling, away over where South Mountain raised its blue-green shoulder. A war. An army. Worse than that, an *enemy* army.

Bodies of troops were divided according to the military plan of the time, first into corps, then into divisions. The divisions were divided into brigades, the brigades into regiments, the regiments into companies; thus it went. Down in Virginia, General Robert E. Lee had decided to invade the North and had sent one of his army corps ahead. Lee was following along behind the shelter of South Mountain. His entire Army of Northern Virginia numbered somewhere between sixty-five and seventy-five thousand men.

Historians differ about the numbers; there is no way to tell accurately now how many soldiers Lee had. Southern records were destroyed at the end of the war, along with much of the city of Richmond, in a huge fire when the Confederate capital surrendered to the North.

It was the Second Corps of Lee's Rebel force, commanded by General Richard S. Ewell, which moved in advance toward Pennsylvania. Ewell was a capable and colorful general. Lee was very fond of him and called him "Dear Dick." Ewell was also brave and had lost a leg in an earlier battle. His admiring soldiers stole a shiny carriage from a Yankee stable, just as the Northerners stole things later on in the South when General William T. Sherman marched through Georgia. In this carriage they installed their respected general, and Ewell rode proudly, one hand resting on his wooden leg. Later, when the battle developed at Gettysburg, Ewell could not very well travel into the fray in this carriage. It was safer and wiser for him to go on horseback, and so he did.

A tale is told: Ewell rode with his staff officers along a Gettysburg highway. They were coming in under the Yankee fire; the bullets squeaked above. Suddenly there was the telltale thud, the awful sound of a bullet ripping into solid substance.

The officers turned in alarm toward their commander. "The general's been hit!" someone cried.

"Gentlemen," piped Ewell in his thin, nervous voice, "it don't hurt a mite to get shot in your wooden leg!"

But this lucky hit would occur in the following

9

week and not now, not while invaders crushed north through Maryland and into the rich gold and green of Pennsylvania.

The long arm of the Rebel cavalry reached into Chambersburg, and immediately the State of Pennsylvania was in an uproar. This was not the first time Chambersburg, twenty-five miles northwest of Gettysburg, had heard the thud of enemy hoofs. The year before, the famous cavalry leader Jeb Stuart and his gray riders had come dashing across the boundary on a raid. The fires they'd set in Chambersburg had burned with brilliance. But Gettysburg had seen no galloping Confederates in 1862, nor had other towns to the north and east. Stuart and his men had turned south at the tiny village of Cashtown and melted away toward Virginia through the valleys of Maryland.

Now this was a different situation in June of 1863. As Southern troopers trotted into the quiet streets of Chambersburg they were the mere forerunners of a more powerful host: brigade after brigade of infantry; columns of wagons creaking and growling under the weight of plunder the Rebels had already stolen—or in some cases had paid for with the thin Confederate scrip which was worth nothing in Pennsylvania.

Granaries had been looted, kegs of beef and pickled pork loaded on the wagons; the wagons themselves had been wrenched from groaning Pennsylvania Dutch farmers. Many of the very horses which strained in harness had been impressed from Yankee pastures. It takes a great deal of food to quiet the appetites of an army. The Rebels did not intend to starve themselves as they looked on the fat lands of their foes.

Governor Andrew Curtin issued a hasty proclamation, crying on loyal Pennsylvanians to rise and defend their State. There were no telephones in the land as yet, but telegraph instruments stuttered in every large city, and brought an especial terror to Harrisburg, the State capital.

In Gettysburg the *clang clang* of a fire alarm went resounding through brick-lined streets and shivered the leaves of chestnut trees. Who was ringing that fire bell? An elderly man: his name was John Burns.

As a boy he had fought the British in the War of 1812; it was said that later he fought against the Seminoles, and in the Mexican War. He had always been military-minded. In his calm, leathery-faced old age, his eyes still glared hard and keen. John Burns was a shoemaker by profession, and lately had found a new local glory when he was named to be constable at Gettysburg. He had hoped to join the armies that went against the South in 1861, but recruiting sergeants shook their heads: he was too old to be a soldier.

For a while Burns served as a teamster, driving wagons for the Federal forces. Then someone in command decided that John was too old for even such service and sent him home. The shiny badge of a constable brought little comfort to the old man's warlike spirit. What was there for a constable to do in a sleepy town like this? Nothing much, except to wear his badge.

But now, with an enemy force roaring through the very next county, John Burns's eyes glinted and his jaw was set. His muscles strained as he sent the brazen clamor of the fire alarm echoing from the cemetery to Oak Ridge and out to the Poor Farm on the north.

Others felt the challenge of the hour. Many of them were boys—gawky students whose ink-smudged noses were usually buried in copybooks at Penn College. Militia companies had been organized some time before, as a gesture toward the National defense. Squads had been drilling after school hours in vacant lots and on wider lawns of the town.

Among them were thin-necked youngsters—boys with wrists too long for their jacket sleeves and not a scrap of beard yet formed on their round chins. There were the lame or the partially lame, and some older fellows . . . this one had heart trouble, perhaps; that one had a tubercular cough; the next might have a hernia or a club-foot. Such ailments or weaknesses had prevented these people from taking the bold place they longed to take, when the first troops went marching off to war. But this was different. They thought of heroes of the past and wanted to be like them.

They stood in their ranks as they had stood in early disordered drills. A man named Major Haller came to swear them into service. Smaller children gaped open-mouthed as their cousins or brothers trooped away to assemble with other raw recruits at Harrisburg. They would become Company A of a strange organization which would be known as the 26th Pennsylvania Emergency Regiment.

Rumors raced from yard to yard. They were wild and frightening and—often—extremely silly tales. Every war breeds its crazy falsehoods, and this summer campaign was no exception.

Ja, said breathless old men and women from neighboring houses, speaking in their dialect; the Rebels were not men. *Nein*, they were beasts. They butchered the calves, they stole the pigs; they had long hair like frontiersmen, and all talked an outlandish language. They would murder anyone, man or woman or child, who got in their way. Worse than that, they would cut off people's ears; they would take their scalps like savages of a century before.

Ja, they would torture even children! Wild and ferocious were the Rebels. *Ach*. Everyone prayed they would not come to Gettysburg.

Today a medium-sized town in Montana has a main street very like that of a medium-sized town in Texas. The eighth grade in a Vermont school is very like the eighth grade in a North Carolina school. In these days of constant communication it is difficult to believe how ignorant many Americans were of the ways of other Americans little more than one hundred twenty years ago. These people had no radios, no movies, no television; even the newspapers were few and far between, and only two or three magazines circulated largely over the country.

The cotton farmer of Alabama lived a life remote from that of the woodsman of Michigan. Neither knew much about the other, not what he ate nor how he did his work.

It is ignorance which breeds our lies; and so it was in 1863. Terrified Pennsylvanians told and believed queer tales about the oncoming Rebels, not only because they were afraid, but also because few of them had ever seen a Southerner or even bothered to guess what one was like.

When Rebel troops reached the North and saw the awe with which people regarded them, they were quick to take advantage of it. Most of the Southern soldiers were young, they were hearty, and they liked to joke.

There is a story that a trooper in Confederate gray, with his tattered hat and dusty boots and big revolver holsters, stood at the door of a Pennsylvania Dutch kitchen and requested food. The women glowered. "Go away," they said. They had no food for Rebels.

The Southerner sighed and gazed across at the cradle where a contented pink-faced baby lay taking its nap. Too bad, said the Rebel—he was mighty hungry. And if they didn't have any other food— Well, he hadn't ever eaten any *baby* meat— not lately at least. But if he had to, why—

Shrieks of the women rang through the room. They tumbled all over each other as they hastened to set out the best from their pantry: head-cheese and doughnuts and pickles and pies and jellies and everything else they could lay their hands on. The young Confederate had never eaten such a meal. He ate it with a twinkle in his eye.

Nevertheless, that soldier had his share in building up such alarms among the inhabitants. Who can say, when one is terribly frightened, where the truth leaves off and the lie begins?

People were fleeing like mad. They dumped themselves and their children and their cats and dogs and chickens and silver spoons into any cart handy, and went rocking away to the north and east.

Gettysburg citizens stared wildly at queer caravans of dusty refugees, and many began to think of running away themselves. Their local militia, weak and ill-shaped as it was, had been the only thing around to protect them from barbaric foes. Now the militia was gone away to Harrisburg. Left to guard the town was no one of much consequence except John Burns, the constable with his ancient musket. No one thought that he could do very much.

Over on Baltimore Street two young women peeped from the window of a brick double-house. Perhaps they wondered if they too should flee, yet they could not. They were the Wade sisters. The elder was married to a chap named McClellan, who was off somewhere with the Federal Army. Young Mrs. John McClellan could not go anywhere; she was about to have a baby; of course her sister would stay with her.

Their names, strangely enough, were Georgia and Virginia—the names of two of the States from which had come whole brigades of this menacing army tramping and rumbling closer along roads from the west.

2

GRAY MEN IN TOWN

Rain threatened in the early evening of Thursday, June 25; the moon was small behind clouds. Gettysburg people crept forth in surprise as they heard the mutter of drums and the thin music of a fife approaching from the direction of the York Pike.

What was this martial music? It could not be the Rebels. The Secessionist army was toward the west, and this approach came from the east. People saw a column of men with guns and knapsacks; they began to recognize familiar shapes and figures. This was Company A of the 26th Emergency Regiment, come home to Gettysburg again.

When the company halted in the town's square, called the Diamond, folks learned that the muster of men at Harrisburg had been completed the previous Monday. On Wednesday the regiment had set out under orders to fend off any Confederate advance in this direction.

It would have been ridiculous had it not been so sad. There were about seven hundred fifty youths and invalids in that regiment, many of them with only two days of training. They were being sent to attack a seasoned, bitter, veteran army of thousands. Those enemies thronging beyond the hills were the same men who had whipped the Northern Army of the Potomac less than two months before, at Chancellorsville.

The majority of the Confederates had seen at least two years of service. They were rangy, powerful men who knew every trick of campaigning amid woods and waters. They could sleep comfortably through rainstorms while rolled in a single tattered blanket. They could creep silently or race in a wild charge with equal ease.

Some Confederate units had been described by foreign observers (professional military men who came over here to watch this war) as the most capable troops ever to go into action. They were better, some said, than French Dragoons or Prussian Guards. Now a bunch of skinny clerks and students were preparing to fight such an enemy!

The Emergency Militia had traveled from Harrisburg on the train. Its cars ran on a railroad that connected Gettysburg with Hanover Junction a few miles to the east, and thus with Baltimore and Philadelphia and the big world outside. As yet the track had not been built west of the town, but a deep cut had been made through Oak Ridge, northwest of Gettysburg beside the Chambersburg Pike. People had grown accustomed to seeing brawny laborers laying ties and bolting iron rails into place.

The new grade was still unsteady and the cars carrying the militia ran off the track when they reached Swift Run, a creek near Gettysburg. Most of the militia camped at the spot. Company A was allowed to proceed on into town for the night, for Gettysburg was home to most of Company A.

It seemed strange to see muskets stacked in front of the stores, to watch gangs of boys, uncertain in their fresh blue uniforms but glad to be wearing them, strolling about the Diamond. They talked largely of punishment they would give the Confederates when they met them. (Such a meeting was only a few hours away, but as yet they didn't know it.)

The next morning the regiment was in column and stumbling west and north along the Chambersburg Pike. Mothers and girlfriends kissed the Gettysburg boys good-bye; children danced beside the armed files until parents called them back. At last the militia moved over the ridge by the Seminary and disappeared in a

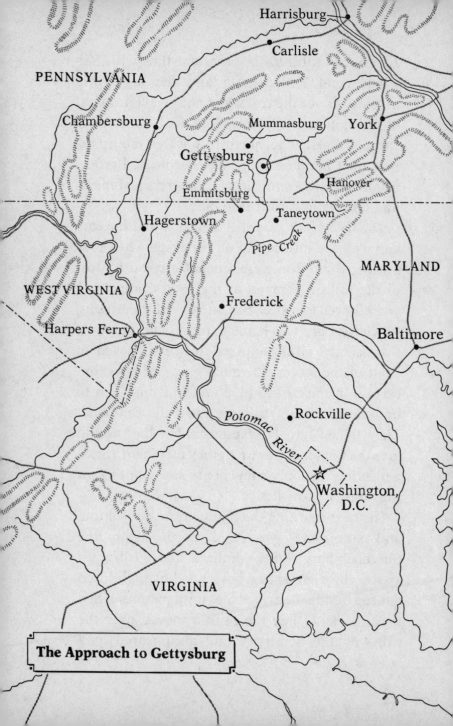

The Approach to Gettysburg

valley beyond. Clouds thickened and came lower; a drizzle began to fall.

It was hours later when, faint and frightening, sounded faraway reports of rifles. The encounter had taken place. It might be called the firing of the first shot at Gettysburg, though this was a mere skirmish compared to later battles.

Secessionist regiments were indeed moving closer, and the little squads of would-be Pennsylvania soldiers had met them at Marsh Creek. The tough Rebel companies swatted them off as if they were mere mosquitoes or fleas.

The 26th Emergency Regiment became, within a matter of minutes, a disorganized mob. Most boys of Company B were captured on the spot; others scattered for their lives. The untrained ranks fired a few shots as they retreated, but many of them had thrown away their guns in terror at the Confederate onslaught. They hid in chicken houses and cob bins. They went scrambling pell-mell through orchards, sobbing for breath as they ran away from Whitmer's farm toward the village of Mummasburg.

Rebels shrugged, wiped scraps of cartridge paper off their lips, slid the slings of their rifles over their shoulders, and went marching on. Shoes—everybody wanted shoes. They had heard that there were some shoe factories in Gettysburg, but the generals and other officers had bigger plans.

Harrisburg, the state capital, waited beyond. And there were York and Columbia and other good-sized towns full of money and manufactured articles so sorely needed by the rural South.

A hundred and fifty Rebel wagons came lurching over the brow of Oak Ridge (during and after the battle it was called Seminary Ridge). The cavalry rode ahead of other units. General J. B. Gordon's brigade of General Jubal A. Early's division hustled along with seeming carelessness. Townspeople peeped warily from behind their shutters and thought of the awful stories they had heard. Would these wild, tanned men kidnap their daughters? Would they actually boil a baby for breakfast? Villagers feared that they should see such horrors occurring before their very eyes.

The week had been hot and, even though it was cooler and rainy today, men can grow very thirsty while marching. Every now and again the Rebels were allowed to break ranks. They poured into the yards and began to work the pump handles. Petunias and larkspurs and nasturtiums were trampled flat as these ragged, hard-faced soldiers clustered around the wells.

General Jubal Early placed a requisition on the town soon after the long gray columns halted in the Diamond. A requisition was an official demand for goods to be supplied to the troops. It seems a little like the act of pirates or bandits to

22

demand food, clothing, and money from unarmed civilians who have no power to resist. Yet that happened on both sides through the entire War Between the States whenever quiet places were invaded.

The demand on this date of Friday, June 26, caused the tight-fisted storekeepers to shudder. Sixty barrels of flour, General Early asked. Seven thousand pounds of pork or bacon, twelve hundred pounds of sugar, six hundred of coffee. Half a ton of salt. Ten bushels of onions; a thousand pairs of shoes, five hundred hats. That was the Confederates' request—all these things to be furnished by the borough of Gettysburg and the county, or else ten thousand dollars in good Federal cash.

Did the Confederates get all these things or the money? They did not. The authorities met and, after a frightened conference, wailed that they did not have such quantities of goods.

There have been different theories about why these first invaders did not enforce their demand with the sword. Captain R. K. Beecham, who fought at Gettysburg and later wrote a book about the battle, insists that the businessmen of Gettysburg had some influence with the enemy. Beecham hints that certain of the small local factories had sold goods to Southern firms before the war. He suggests that many people of this section were heartily in sympathy with the Confederate cause although they pretended to support the North.

Maybe this is true, maybe not. Gettysburg sent many of its sons out to fight for the Union long before the 26th Emergency Regiment was thought of. On the other hand, many Northern communities, especially those near the Mason-Dixon line, had their share of Southern sympathizers. (Just as in remote highlands of the South there were little groups who called themselves "The Right Sort of People" and who supported the Federal government—sometimes at the point of a gun!)

Men of secret Confederate belief in Northern states belonged to an organization called The Knights of the Golden Circle, though their angry Yankee neighbors called them Copperheads. Perhaps this was because the secret badge of the society, concealed somewhere on their persons, was in the shape of an old-fashioned copper cent.

The Knights of the Golden Circle had promised that they would rise in force and assist the Rebels whenever they came charging through the North. But during the several raids that actually occurred the Knights were suspected of hiding under their beds instead.

If persons of concealed Secesh belief did exist in Gettysburg, there was at least one citizen who took violent issue with the Rebels the moment they appeared: old John Burns. He appeared in the Diamond and announced boldly to the leaders that he was going to arrest them for trespassing on United States property.

The confident invaders were amused, but John made them a little angry, too. Promptly they locked him up in the local jail—the very place where John had locked drunkards or thieves on the few occasions when that was necessary. The warlike cobbler languished behind bars until the Rebel force moved on to possess York and other towns to the east; then some citizen came and let him out. Burns was not subdued by his experience; he got hold of a lantern and a horse pistol and set out to arrest any stragglers he found.

Every marching army has stragglers: a few unfortunates, weaker or less spirited than the rest, who leave the ranks to sit exhausted by the roadside and then are unable to catch up with the main force. Sometimes they are deserters who have no desire to face the fighting to come.

Such stragglers as there were, John Burns found. He went prowling behind fences and through empty cellars, and had the satisfaction of locking a few woebegone Rebels in the jail where he had been confined earlier.

But Constable John Burns, cobbler and wagon driver, and the 26th Emergency Regiment were not to be the only uniformed forces to oppose the gray columns approaching Gettysburg. While the Rebel force was spreading and seeking in Pennsylvania, the Northern army was busy far to the south. The Union force in the eastern part of the United States was called the Army of the Potomac and was commanded by General Joseph Hooker. He was a brave soldier, a veteran of long experience—but Hooker was quick-tempered and did not get along well with other military men.

Nearly two months earlier, the Yankees, led by Hooker, had met disaster before a Confederate force, which they outnumbered, at Chancellorsville in Virginia. The general had not been in any condition to direct his officers during important hours of the battle. His friends said that he had been dazed when a shell struck the porch column against which he was leaning. Other people in the army, who didn't like Hooker, declared that he was drunk. Drunk or sober, he was not the world's greatest commander, nor the Nation's. His forces were routed.

Mere bravery is not the only thing needed in order for a man to be a fine military leader. He must have wisdom and patience and imagination, and it does not appear that Joe Hooker was endowed with any lion's share of these qualities.

On the same day that Gordon's brigade pressed through Gettysburg, Hooker's army crossed the Potomac River from Virginia into Maryland. A portion of his troops had already crossed on the day before.

Hooker was in a rage. He had asked General Henry W. Halleck (who was his superior officer as Chief of Staff of the army) for permission to withdraw some troops that served as a garrison at Harpers Ferry, far up the Potomac. Hooker wanted to use these troops to attack Lee's lines of communication stretching down through western Maryland. Halleck, who must go down in history as one of the most obstinate men who ever lived, refused to let General Hooker use the Harpers Ferry soldiers. The two generals quarreled vigorously back and forth at long range. The fuss ended only when Hooker wrote out his resignation as commander.

The new general who followed Hooker was not widely known among Unionists. His name was George Gordon Meade, and he had been born in Spain. He was an American, however—not a Spaniard, as was rumored among the soldiers.

Halleck must have thought that he could get along with Meade better than he had with General Hooker. Promptly he gave orders that the Harpers Ferry garrison could be subject to Meade's orders if Meade wanted them. But the new general decided that he had more important concerns. His main worry was the safety of Washington, the capital of the disunited states.

People in Pennsylvania might very well believe

that Lee sought to capture Harrisburg and Philadelphia. There were even wild notions in some quarters to the effect that the Rebel commander was aiming at New York City. Down in Maryland the loyal citizens feared for the safety of Baltimore. Meade was determined to make sure, first of all, that the Rebel general could not bring his long columns speeding down from the north to seize Washington. He felt that Lee was capable of such a move, once he heard that the Army of the Potomac had crossed the river whose name it bore.

Meade began to spread his army in the shape of a great protective fan between Washington and a possible dangerous advance. He put the First Corps here, the Eleventh Corps there, the Second Corps far to the southeast, and so on. He sent a cavalry division poking out ahead, working its way up through Maryland. The clash would come when the two armies met.

Meade even tried to pick out a proper position on ground of his own choosing. He sent engineers galloping along Pipe Creek, near a place called Taneytown. They reported that the hills in that region would be favorable to the Union defense, if only they could draw the Confederates down to give battle at Pipe Creek. Every general would like to select the ground where he deploys his men for battle. Usually only one of the two opposing commanders is able to do so; sometimes neither of them can.

That is exactly why there was a battle at Gettysburg. Imagine a star with ten or a dozen points. The star is the village of Gettysburg. The points are roads shooting out in all directions: the Fairfield Road, the Chambersburg Pike, the Mummasburg Road, the Carlisle Road, the Harrisburg Road, the York Pike, the Hanover Road, the Baltimore Pike, the Emmitsburg Road, the Taneytown Road. Several of these many highways split themselves into other roads only a few miles beyond Gettysburg.

The Civil War armies, dependent on horses and cumbersome cannon, had to advance to an assembly point by means of established roads. So, when Lee felt the need to concentrate his army, he brought it down from the northeast and north and northwest. At the same time, the Federal army came up from the southeast and south and southwest. All roads seemed to have their ending at Gettysburg. Gettysburg would indeed be the end of the road for thousands of men and boys.

On Friday, June 26, a thin rain was coming down. The damp gray columns had thudded away toward York. Other divisions of Ewell's Second Corps were progressing along other roads, away in the north and the west. The muddy streets of Gettysburg had never looked like this before: the ruts, the marks of horses, the scraps of clothing and equipment lost by gray soldiers or deliberately thrown away in order to lighten their packs.

The wet night was empty, frightening. *Ja*, who knew? Maybe the Rebels would return tomorrow. Earth around the wells was trampled into mush, the pansies and hollyhock plants had been stamped, a gate had been knocked off a fence here and there. An empty wagon stood abandoned, sagging on its broken axle.

In earliest morning eager little boys would venture along the streets, hunting for stray buckles and pistol caps. People gathered to see the wreckage of a railroad bridge which the Rebels had broken to pieces east of town. Freight cars standing along a side track had been burned.

Old ladies shuddered through the evening in their beds, watching the dying flames reflected on clean walls. This must be war in its most dreadful aspect. Still, no babies had been eaten.

But one had arrived in the world. Young Mrs. John McClellan, the former Georgia Wade, had a son born to her in the brick double-house on Baltimore Street, even while Rebel wagons rattled on roads nearby.

Gettysburg people considered themselves lucky and were glad to believe that the enemy had gone—perhaps forever. Little did they know!

3

A SPY AND
A TYRANT

Scattered over the countryside south of Gettysburg were neat little farms. Many of the same houses are there today, surrounded by knobs and cubes of polished marble where monuments stand in quantities. There too a traveler can see today a great horse and rider motionless for all time above a patch of blooming clover. A cluster of sculptured warriors leap, guns in their hands, from a green hillside. . . .

The statues had not been erected on June 30, 1863. The armies which were to inspire them had not yet come. But the armies were close, closer than any drowsy Pennsylvania farmer, intent on his early oats, could believe.

A few days before, the farmers who lived in these houses had listened appalled to stories about foraging parties. When Early's advance resounded on that misty Friday, they had hastened south beside the twisted creeks, driving cattle and horses ahead of them. Along the reaches of Rock Creek or Plum Run, far back amid berry bushes and dogwood trees beyond the boulders of Devil's Den and the Round Tops, herds might be hidden safely. Foragers would find only empty stables and pens if they appeared.

As it happened, not many Confederates went prowling south of the Chambersburg and York Pikes on that first invasion Friday. They picked up horses, they impressed food along the paths by which they marched; but Early was in haste to reach York. Most of the farmers' mares and milch cows cropped the wet grass of unfamiliar ravines quite undisturbed.

Many neighbors brought their stock home on Monday, June 29. There were rumors of vast butternut-colored hordes ranging along the Susquehanna River all the way from Columbia and Wrightsville up toward Harrisburg; but danger seemed to have departed from this immediate neighborhood. It was thought safe to herd the cattle home.

A few people delayed until Tuesday, June 30. Tuesday was very hot. Most of the early summer had been hot in that region. No rain had fallen in several days, and dust lay like talcum powder along ruts where the cartwheels mashed it.

Shadows of lonely trees were bluish, motionless against the green hay; insects twitched with itchy midsummer sounds in the ranks of weeds. It was a weary day, this Tuesday, to go hunting for cows and calves already half wild from their wanderings.

An old local story describes an ignorant farmer and his little boy, herding their cows north along the Emmitsburg Road. Dust puffed like smoke from the animals' hoofs as they walked or trotted in alarm and tried to shy loose through gateways along the road. Other dust came pounding from the south. It made a cloud around armed men on horses, men who had great sabers strapped beside their legs, whose staring eyes were like holes in their masks of sweat and dirt.

More Rebels? The farmer and his boy shook in their fright. *Stay close by Papa, Henry.*

The squad of riders loomed around. These were "videttes." The farmer might not know the word, but it meant that these were stray cavalrymen sent out ahead of the main body of troops, scouting highways and byways, making sure that no ambush awaited.

With relief the farmer and his child understood the color of the cavalrymen's jackets, the reassuring paler blue of their breeches with yellow stripes on the sides. Federals, National troops? *Ja*, they were Yankees. . . . The scouts asked a few questions.... No, there were no Confederates anywhere in the neighborhood. They had all gone, days before.

The cavalrymen turned back to report to their officers while the Pennsylvanians scuttled to safety with their calves. *Ja*, the Yankee army was coming, but who knew? Maybe Yankees would wish to steal a good horse or a fine fat cow just as the Rebels had done.

Ground along the Emmitsburg Road trembled in that glaring afternoon. A dust cloud of mighty proportions rose flat through the length of the valley. It brought with it a division of mounted men, thousands, with all the necessary wagons— the heavy small carts loaded with iron and tubs of anvils, carts in which the farriers rode. (Farriers were blacksmiths. Horseshoes were important to the cavalry.)

Again the pumps squeaked, the windlasses swung above wayside wells. Flowers were trampled once more. Women and girls came out, pulling aprons over their heads to shield their gaze from the glaring sun. They heard the neighing and thud and jingle and rattle of the 1st Division, Cavalry Corps, Army of the Potomac. It was commanded by General John Buford, Jr.

Meade had sent this division up to Gettysburg, hoping to find where the main strength of the enemy was gathered or could be assembled.

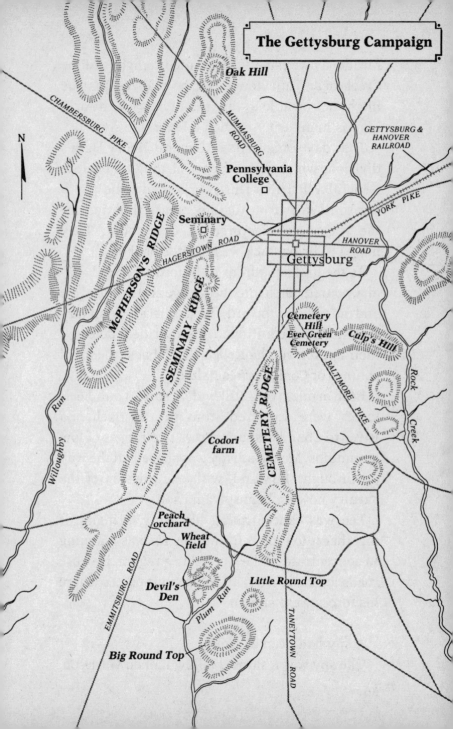

Meade, as we have seen, wanted to fight at Pipe Creek near Taneytown; but he realized that he might not be able to lure the Rebels into attacking his main army in such a favorable spot.

That day some units of General Henry Heth's division, which formed part of the Confederate General A. P. Hill's Third Corps, had come grinding southeast from Chambersburg, hunting for the shoes manufactured at Gettysburg. They hoped to bring back wagonloads of shoes.

As the first squadrons of Buford's Federal cavalry poured north into the village and swung west and northwest toward the Lutheran Seminary and McPherson's Ridge, gray outriders detected their approach. The Rebels faded back; the main column of Confederates halted.

Both armies were still widely spread out. Lee's forces were scattered from the Susquehanna River to Chambersburg across two ranges of low mountains. Meade's army was spaced all the way up through Maryland, with one division of the cavalry now on Pennsylvania soil.

Lee was concentrating his army, bringing it together into tighter formation. He was planning to concentrate in the Gettysburg region, because roads led there from all the distant places where his forces were strewn.

A spy had been at work.

The spy was a shrewd fellow named Harrison,

who served at this time usually under direct orders of General James Longstreet, commanding Lee's First Corps. Before the Secessionists moved out of Virginia, Longstreet sent for Harrison and gave him a purse of money—not flimsy paper bills of the South, but solid gold coins.

With this fund for expenses, Harrison was ordered to put on citizen's clothes and slip into the city of Washington. There he was to wander at will, seeking the company of Union officers in bars and billiard parlors, in cafés and in the smoking rooms of big hotels. He was to act the part of a good-natured, inquiring, friendly, patriotic citizen.

He could pretend that he came to Washington to seek an appointment with his own congressman or senator. He was to keep his eyes and ears open and try, if possible, to learn the position and plans of the Union army. Once he had discovered such information, he was to report back to Longstreet.

Harrison said, "But, sir, how will I ever find your headquarters? General Lee is planning to invade the North, and you might be anywhere. Could you tell me where I might meet you on such-and-such a date?"

Longstreet felt that it would not be wise for Harrison to have any detailed knowledge of the Confederate plans. Harrison was going into the enemy capital, and he might be captured. There was no telling how severely the Yankees would question him in such a case.

"No," said Longstreet, "my command is large enough for you to find it easily. You'll hear reports and rumors; people will be talking about nothing else but our invasion. Move cautiously. You can find me."

General Longstreet in his memoirs describes Harrison as a *scout*, but *spy* is a much better word. Any man who wore civilian clothes instead of a uniform and crept about through the towns of his enemies, searching for vital information, was most certainly a spy and subject to be shot at once if caught.

Harrison, however, was not caught. He was a smallish man of athletic build. Longstreet describes him as having hazel eyes, a brown beard, with dark hair and dark complexion. He was not outstanding in appearance—just a simple type of fellow who might readily win the confidence of unwise officers, especially if their tongues were loosened by drink.

We can imagine Harrison strolling into a bar at a Washington hotel, standing aloof, ordering a drink, observing the chatter and laughter of a major and two captains near him. An arm is jostled, a word is passed; an apology. Soon more glasses are filled. Men talk about the war, about General Hooker. . . .

Harrison was clever. There he stood, with the hangman's noose around his neck, and any slip on his part would tighten the knot. He didn't slip: a very valuable man to the Rebel cause indeed.

The days passed, and the nights. In secret Harrison examined the information he had gleaned. Washington was not far from any spot where the various Union army corps moved or waited. And people talked too much about matters which should have been military secrets.

Like a shadow the slim Harrison eased himself out of Washington and tramped away through the night. It was child's play for him to avoid sentries. He halted each day in the neighborhood of troops if he could, and thus he heard more talk.

On the night of June 28, Harrison had traveled all the way across Maryland and into Pennsylvania, where the gossip of a hundred Marylanders told him that the Confederate forces had gone. Longstreet was at Chambersburg, resting his troops briefly; Harrison found him.

Harrison recited the positions where he believed the Yankees to be: three corps of the Union army near Frederick, Maryland; others moving northward. Years afterward Longstreet wrote that he considered Harrison's information more accurate than any which might have been gained from scouting activity by the Rebels' own cavalry.

The First Corps commander sent his spy on to General Lee to report immediately. He also sent a note suggesting to the Commander in Chief that it might be wise to gather the Army of Northern Virginia together in order to prepare for a battle. Lee agreed and gave the necessary orders.

Division after division, the gray invaders rose and began to march. Gettysburg was the logical place for them to gather. All roads seemed to lead to Gettysburg.

The main highways for the space of a hundred miles through this rolling farmland of the middle East became jammed with troops—both Union and Confederate. Heavy wheels of cannon crunched, vast numbers of horses left their mark, the soldiers walked. Few of them traveled in comfort. Many, if they did not have good officers, traveled with angry hearts and in misery.

There was, for example, Colonel Edward E. Cross, commanding a brigade in Hancock's Second Corps of the Union army. Veterans have recorded in diaries or letters the hatred they bore for Colonel Cross. During the advance toward Gettysburg, Cross was seen beating a soldier of the 148th Pennsylvania Infantry with his sword. He was a cruel man who issued unnecessary orders merely because he had the power to do so.

A soldier's feet are very nearly the most important portions of his body. The blister, the stone bruise, the sore chafing of a shoe: these spell worse misery to a tired warrior than any common degree of starvation or danger. If the stiff leather of an old-fashioned army shoe became drenched and then dried, it hardened into a misery like iron. All wise marchers took pains not to wet their shoes if they could avoid it.

At one point some Union regiments were moving toward a stream directly on their front. Here there was no wide wagon bridge—only a narrow foot bridge, the width of a single log, laid across the stream. Men could not march on such a bridge in regular formation, by threes or fours or twos. They had to go single file; they had to turn aside a little in order to do it. They were progressing rapidly dry-shod across the stream, glad for the service of even a bridge like this, when an angry voice smote the air.

It was Colonel Cross. He had ridden up to see them turning aside; he glared and snapped at them:

"Why are you men falling out of formation?"

"Sir, this bridge—there's only room for one."

"Get back over there the way you were headed. Get into column. Forward, march!"

He watched sternly while the long column paced once more to the creekside through mud, splashing, stumbling over rocks, and up again through more mud on the other side. The soldiers were doomed to suffer the rest of the day in a stiff, damp torture of shoes that dried slowly, caked in deep dust of the road, slowing their legs as they moved, opening fresh blisters and old sores.

It would have been far more sensible for Colonel Cross to allow his troops to use the little bridge. They would have been a better fighting unit if they had marched dry-shod. They would have been less worn-out when they reached their destination, less subject to the ills of foot infection—sturdier soldiers in every way.

Cross went to his death at Gettysburg. There were rumors afterward that he had been shot by his own men. Probably this was not true. Colonel Cross was brave in battle, no matter what faults he owned; he had been wounded many times. The Confederate fire scorched thick on that farm where he fell.

General Buford set up his headquarters at the seminary the night of June 30, but he spent little time in sleep. His Union troopers had reported gray forces only a few miles up the pike. Seminary Ridge was a good strong ridge. The Confederates would try to grab it in the morning: Buford was confident of that.

Anxiously he wondered at what time the First Corps, marching on foot more slowly behind him, would reach this village. It was a hot night, and there was a moon. Buford and his staff rode far and wide, scouting the area.

To the west, amid the shadows along Marsh Creek, the nearest Confederates pondered upon the presence of these Yankees. Probably just some cavalry militia, the Rebs thought. They could be easily pushed aside in the morning.

They were not pushed aside with ease. During the first hours they were not pushed aside at all.

Buford's pickets rubbed against the Confederates soon after sunrise, Wednesday, July 1. The battle started in earnest about eight A.M., when General Heth's Confederate division began its grueling advance toward the region.

At first thought it might seem that a band of infantry would not stand a fair chance against a party of cavalry, but the reverse was true. Cavalrymen, mounted on their horses, presented too much of a target for the enemy rifles. In a case like this it was necessary for them to dismount and let a certain number of men take charge of the horses. The rest of the troopers fought on the ground, shielding themselves behind trees and rocks and fences, just as their foes were doing.

Buford found pride in the determined conduct

of his men, but he knew they could not hold out forever against the increasing numbers of Confederates who swept in.

When the fight developed, Buford sent a rider rushing down the Emmitsburg Road with an urgent message to General John F. Reynolds, commanding the Federal First, Third, and Eleventh Corps, the right wing of the Army of the Potomac. Numbers would be needed to stop numbers. Reynolds would know whether it was wisest to have the surviving cavalrymen fall back toward the safety of the main Yankee force or to throw in other troops as soon as possible.

Buford trusted that Reynolds would hasten forward in person, speeding ahead of his command, to look over the situation. He climbed into the cupola of the seminary and surveyed the battle from this vantage point. He hoped that Reynolds would hurry. Noise of the Yankee carbines, volleys of Confederate muskets rose into a storm.

4

THREE MEN NAMED JOHN

The popular commander is not always the best commander, but General Reynolds of the Union Army was both. A quiet-faced, bearded man in early middle-age, he was a veteran of the Mexican War and of Indian expeditions out West. He liked to work with young soldiers, and they gave him devotion and respect because he earned it.

Reynolds was commanding at the West Point Military Academy when the war broke out, and he went on active duty that same year. For a time he had been a prisoner of the Confederates but was exchanged and went back into service. He had commanded the First Corps for nine months now.

Reynolds rode, powdered with hot dust of the highway. He brought his big horse up the slope, bending low in the saddle to avoid branches of the apple trees. There was an orchard just below the seminary.

Buford had come down from the cupola and was on the steps waiting for him. They faced each other, the two Johns: Buford the one-starred brigadier general, Reynolds the two-starred major general. Hundreds of carbines were banging steadily nearby. The sound of the reports began to change; the cavalrymen were running out of ammunition for their carbines and were forced to draw their revolvers. (The sound of a Colt's revolver is different from that of a long-barreled gun.)

Historians have recorded the exact words of the two, overheard by an officer who stood near.

The bearded John Reynolds called to John Buford, "What's the matter, John?"

Buford hurried down the seminary steps. "There's hell to pay. They jumped me first thing this morning, General. Is that your folks coming from Emmitsburg?" He pointed off south where the advance of more troops was building a dust cloud.

Reynolds nodded. "The First Corps. They're on the road. I can get Wadsworth"—one of his division commanders—"up here in short order, behind this ridge we're on. Do you think you can hold out until his infantry is in line?"

"Reckon I can."

Buford was from Kentucky; his speech showed it. He used the rather informal, easy manner of talk which was native to him.

One of Buford's officers, Colonel Devin, had bragged early that morning before the Rebel attack began: "I'll take care of all the enemy that will attack my front in the next twenty-four hours."

"No, you won't take care of them, Tom," John Buford had replied. "They'll attack you this morning, and they'll come a-booming when they come—skirmishers three deep. You watch! You'll have to fight like the devil to hold out until supports get here."

The next few hours proved how right Buford was.

The Union infantry units could not be lifted into the fray by any magic means. They were coming as fast as they could, but they were still a long way down the valley. The two generals walked among the scattered trees to examine the lines thoroughly.

Reynolds was a soldier's general. He understood the tiresome roads, the long marches, the rough pebbles which got into men's shoes, the welcome halt at last. Sometimes such a halt for rest would be made in a woodland where trees offered shade. Reynolds always tried to halt his command in woods if he could; so did many others. But he was more considerate than most.

How often, during such a rest, the men would long for a quick cup of coffee. They would start a fire, put a tin can—or an old burnt coffeepot tied to their packs—over the blaze. The men would stir in the coffee grounds, watching anxiously, hoping against hope that the coffee would boil long enough for them to taste its strength, that they would be halted long enough for the liquid to cool to the point where they could drink it.

But too often the bugles would start clamoring under the trees, aides would ride quickly along the road, motioning company commanders into column again. The blazing twigs would be scattered, the steaming water and precious brown grounds tossed upon the coals. Men would swing away, coffee-less, hating all commanders with a blind hate which only poor foot-weary infantrymen could know.

But this didn't happen to soldiers marching under the command of John Reynolds. If he halted the troops and no word was passed to boil coffee, they simply didn't start any coffee. No use to go through a lot of work for nothing. It was foolish to waste the precious brown grains that were so hard to come by. So when General John Reynolds knew that regiments must move on in a hurry, he said nothing. But if it were possible at all, Reynolds, far at the head of the files, would swing his booted leg over the saddle and step down on the grass. He would speak quickly to an aide.

"Go tell the commanders to tell their men that there'll be time to boil coffee."

The corps would not move until coffee had been boiled and had drained down those thousands of eager throats. The corps would not move because Reynolds promised that it would not.

The First Corps of the Union Army of the Potomac came bursting from the Emmitsburg Road, trotting through heat waves of the pastures. Advance squads tore at the rails, dissolving fences in their path so that regiments could pass through. Wisconsin and Michigan men they were—the Iron Brigade, so called—and famous throughout the army because they wore black hats instead of caps. These were the same black hats in which they had been mustered as inexperienced militiamen. Now they were experienced and hardy.

The Iron Brigade knew its job. General Reynolds galloped along the slope to give final orders to General Solomon Meredith, the brigade commander. The dark line spread through the trees. Orders were yelled.

The tired cavalrymen of Buford's command were glad to see the black-hatted infantry coming. They had been fighting for hours, unused to this kind of warfare; most of their ammunition pouches were empty.

As for the Confederates beyond McPherson's Ridge, they would find an unpleasant truth in the appearance of those hated black hats on their front. They had believed, up to this point, that they were confronted only by Pennsylvania militia. But here came big lumbermen and miners from the Great Lakes, pounding toward them down the slope. Annoyed Southern voice after annoyed Southern voice cried, "That ain't no militia. Look at them old black hats! It's the Army of the Potomac, sure."

"Have a care. Please, sir, take a little care!" Buford kept pleading with General Reynolds. The general was racing to and fro with no regard for his own safety. His only concern was the battle and the troops he must manage. Should he send General Cutler over to the right? There was that railroad excavation. Should he hold the 2nd Division in reserve? Again he would ride to an open point on the ridge and aim his glasses toward the west.

Somewhere off among those low willows an unknown, unnamed sharpshooter in gray did the job he was supposed to do. He was poking his rifle carefully through the brush, firing at any favorable distant target which showed. General Reynolds appeared in his sights, a dark blue figure tiny and far away. The Confederate might not have known who this man was; probably he never knew; he himself may have been killed a few minutes later.

There was the sound of the bullet slapping. The general toppled from his saddle and lay motionless on the grass. There was a blue hole in the skin behind Reynolds's right ear, another hole on the left side of his head. The bullet had drilled cleanly through his skull, and so he was one of the first to die.

Out past the dust of the Chambersburg Pike, across heated, sloping fields, into the shade of sparse, low oaks, walked old John Burns, the constable. He had a habit of squinting; now he squinted more than ever as he saw smoke thickening ahead. The common powder for Civil War guns was black, and when it exploded within the barrel a great deal of smoke puffed out. If a hundred men fired their guns, there was soon a cloud amid the bushes.

In this battle thousands were shooting at each other as rapidly as they could ram their torn paper-cartridges down the muzzles and fasten their caps. A few newly invented guns were in use during this battle, even some with brass cartridges; but John Burns carried one of the oldest guns of all. It was an ancient smoothbore musket with a bit of flint fastened to the hammer. The flint would fall against an upright piece of steel.

There would be a spark; a little powder would puff with flame and burn through a hole into the barrel of the gun itself. The bullet would be fired out. That was the way the oldest guns worked. But the majority of the soldiers had percussion-cap guns, which seemed to them much more modern than the weapon lugged along by this angry civilian.

Slightly wounded soldiers limped across pastures below the seminary. Other able-bodied troops rushed about on military errands. These young men stared, amazed, at the constable plodding toward the battle. A few halted to question him, to urge that he return to safety in the village.

John Burns shook his head. He had been waiting for this moment. For two years he had been angry at the rebellious Southerners who he believed sought to wreck his country.

"You'll get hit," the blue-clad youths cried.

"Don't care if I do."

"You're just an old man. You don't know how to fight."

"Yes, I've fit before," John Burns told them. "Fit the British long ago, with a gun like this." He slapped the brown musket with his gnarled hand.

A soldier yelled, "Here, take this cartridge pouch and put the strap over your shoulder. At least you'll look like a soldier, with this."

John Burns had a gleaming powder horn; he touched his pocket to show where he carried his bullets. "I don't care about newfangled things. Don't know how to handle them. I can get bullets out of my pocket easy enough."

On he went up the slope, the booming of battle coming to meet him. He didn't mind the teasing of these lads. Most of them were young enough to be his grandchildren. He thought only of the Rebels. They had made fun of him the previous Friday—had shoved him around, locked him in his own jail.

And his cows! John Burns explained about the cows as he halted beside other soldiers to wipe his hot forehead with a wet handkerchief. After General Early's visit Burns found that some of his cows were gone. The Rebels had driven them off—later to butcher them, no doubt, into fresh beefsteak. The ones they hadn't driven off the Rebels had milked without so much as a by-your-leave. They needed to be taught a lesson, and the grim-faced cobbler-constable believed that he was just the man to teach it.

He found more than jeers and pestering as he trudged past the troopers who guarded the empty-saddled horses of Buford's cavalry. He found respect and even help in his strange little campaign. The boys were all agreed about one thing:

Burns's gun was too clumsy; it would not shoot far enough. Reluctantly he placed the weapon and powder horn in a clump of bushes. He'd get these things later, he said, if they hadn't been stolen.

From a wounded soldier, hobbling toward the rear, he accepted the rifle and cartridge pouch which the boy pressed on him.

Colonel Langhorne Wister, commander of the 150th Pennsylvania, took a moment off from his duties to give the old man a word of advice. "Better stay here in the woods with us," said Wister. "There's more shelter here."

This was still too far away from the enemy to suit John Burns. He wanted to go closer. Other soldiers were out ahead and to the left—men of the Iron Brigade. Among these crouching warriors Burns found contentment at last. And the Yankee soldiers said later that they took courage in his presence; they found comfort in knowing he was near.

Long, long before he had fought . . . as a boy in his teens, and hundreds of miles away. He had been at Plattsburg . . . Lundy's Lane. That was where General Winfield Scott had achieved his first fame, and Scott had grown as huge in reputation as he was in body. He had been commander of the whole United States Army during the Mexican War. Now Winfield Scott, sick and pulpy with great age, was in retirement. But John

Burns was still able to do a constable's job, and on this fine hot day an infantryman's job too.

He slid behind a tree, for he knew enough to take cover. He loaded this strange new gun. He squinted at the sight; he watched for a target. He did not blaze away foolishly like a raw recruit.

Some of these young soldiers fighting in this war got so rattled that they didn't even know when their guns misfired. So the charge would be in the barrel still; and they'd ram in a fresh cartridge on top of that, and then maybe another and another. Sometimes at last, when the cap didn't misfire but connected with the powder instead, the whole gun would blow up like a bursting shell in the frightened soldier's hands.

But Burns knew better than to go hog-wild. He'd be patient, take his time, use his wits and his eyes. He didn't know these boys he was fighting beside, but they seemed a good sort. Their colonel, a man named Robinson—7th Wisconsin—was impressed by John Burns because John was so obviously a veteran. Robinson let the old soldier fight alongside his men.

More Confederates pressed on the Iron Brigade front. Great bodies of Southern troops sped to the growing battle from Chambersburg, from Mummasburg, from Carlisle. It was obvious that the Unionists were outnumbered and sorely pressed.

Away over to the right, north of Gettysburg,

the Eleventh Corps had arrived and was in defensive position. Already they were being assailed on their front by masses of gray-clad soldiers. The sharp, pungent smell of burnt powder ringed the town and drifted through the streets.

The Confederates had only three corps in the battle during the three days of fighting. By the end of the second day, the entire Army of the Potomac was present on the Federal side: seven corps. That sounds as if the Rebels had less than half as many men as the Yankees; but it was not that way.

In the Southern army, when men of a regiment died or went to the hospital or were captured, other men were promptly put into their places in that same regiment. It was a good plan, as the record shows. An inexperienced soldier fights more willingly if he has a veteran on either side of him. Thus, regiments were kept at very near their original strength until the Confederacy began to fall apart. Of course, that meant that brigades and divisions and army corps were also filled up to their proper numbers.

But in the Northern army, new recruits went into brand-new regiments. The older battered regiments, weakened by death and wounds, didn't have their ranks filled up. A thousand men had enlisted originally, perhaps, in each regiment of the Philadelphia Brigade; yet when the Philadelphia Brigade of the Second Corps reached Gettysburg they numbered only about a thousand men in all the four regiments.

Thus, the three Confederate corps mustered perhaps seventy thousand men to begin with at Gettysburg. The seven corps of the Northern Army mustered perhaps eighty-five thousand. No one is sure of the exact figures, though people have spent years arguing. As a whole, the Rebels were certainly outnumbered by the third day; but on the first day the Confederates had the weight of numbers on their own side.

Matters like this were of no concern to John Burns. He crouched behind his tree, watching the advance of enemies on his front, firing until his gun grew nearly too hot to hold. The 7th Wisconsin received orders to withdraw from this position; there was too much pressure here; they must deploy to the right. They moved off, but the constable did not go with them.

"I never saw John Burns after our movement to the right," wrote Sergeant George Eustice after the war. "I only know that he was true blue and grit to the backbone, and fought until he was three times wounded."

5

THE YANKEES
RUN

The Civil War brought a change in the manner of dressing the troops—*uniforming* would be a better word. That is what *uniforms* really means: "suits of clothes all alike." In ancient times men went to battle in whatever rude garments they happened to be wearing. When each leader finally decided that his own men should dress alike, they were said to be wearing *uniform* clothing.

Back at the beginning of the nineteenth century, when Napoleon led his invaders through Europe, there were many different styles of dress in the same army. You may have seen Highlanders or at least pictures of them. The different Scottish families each wore a different color of the kilt; thus in time each regiment wore kilts of a certain pattern. So it was with other nations. In

England the Guards would have coats, hats, and ornaments of a certain style. The Light Infantry would wear something else again.

The United States copied European styles in its navy and army. For instance, American soldiers once wore helmets with little spikes on top, just like the German soldiers in World War I. And Americans have worn blue, they have worn buff or brown, and pale khaki, red, green, pink, uniforms of mixed blue and khaki—all sorts of colors of dress.

At the outbreak of the Civil War the United States had only a small army, and many of the officers resigned in order to serve with troops of the seceding States. The vast divisions which swarmed from Kentucky to the Atlantic Ocean, from Missouri to the Gulf, were mostly composed of men who enlisted hastily. They had never fought before, were not even trained to fight, and got their only training on disordered battlefields. They came from a thousand neighborhoods and towns.

They were, to begin with, known by local names: the Joe Daviess Guards, the Washington Artillery, the Black Horse Troop. Thus, being locally recruited and formed, there was not much similarity in their appearance. Each regiment, sometimes each company, would be clad differently. Troops from the South often wore blue, those in the Northern army sometimes had gray uniforms. There were the Fire Zouaves—members of local fire brigades who decided to enlist together. The first regiment of these adopted the fez, white gaiters, and baggy trousers of African troops serving with the French army. There was even a regiment of Highlanders from New York City, wearing their plaids and marching away to the music of bagpipes.

As a result, there was quite a mix-up in the first big battle, which occurred near the town of Manassas, along a creek named Bull Run in northern Virginia in the summer of 1861. Friends fired on friends. Troops advanced through smoke and could not be identified as friends or foes until they were practically within the lines. Hodgepodge regiments turned their guns against adjoining regiments of the same brigade.

Even the flags which were carried into battle didn't help much. The official Confederate flag was red, white, and blue—just like the national flag—but it had only three stripes instead of thirteen. However, it too had a field of blue in the upper corner. From a distance it very closely resembled the banner of our Nation rather than that of the eleven states which had pulled out of the Union.

Several times during that angry day, along rolling valleys southwest of Washington, the Confederates attacked each other by mistake. So it came about that a new flag was designed: the Confederate battle flag—all bright red, with diagonal lines of stars crossing in the middle, much like the St. Andrew's cross of old Scotland. This is the flag commonly described today as the flag of the dead Confederacy. Sometimes it is mistakenly called the Stars and Bars. But the Stars and Bars, the official Southern flag, is not displayed often.

Grim experience can change a previous custom. By the third year of war the troops looked a good deal alike. There were minor variations as to cavalry, artillery, and so on, but in the main the uniform of the South was gray, that of the North blue. Gone were the fancy leggings of the Zouaves, the bright cockades of home-raised regiments. Gone were the odd-looking havelocks— little capes which the men used to attach to their caps to cover neck and shoulders and supposedly ward off sunstroke.

In fact, by 1862 things were beginning to be a little *too* uniform to be convenient. There was no way, in a hurry and at a distance, to tell which brigade or corps was which—no way to tell a higher-ranking officer from one of lower rank. Often there was no way to tell an officer from an enlisted man. (You have to be quite close in order to see the difference between bars or leaves or other tiny insignia of rank.)

Badges to mark the members of divisions and regiments were introduced by a bold Northern general named Phil Kearny. He had commanded a division when the Yankees attempted to capture Richmond in 1862. Before that he had served abroad and picked up many ideas from the Europeans. The dashing Phil Kearny, who had only one arm but galloped like a cowboy into battle just the same, invented a badge for his division.

He ordered everyone to cut out little pieces of red flannel in the shape of a diamond. High-ranking officers wore this diamond on top of their caps. Lieutenants and captains wore it on the front of their caps. The sergeants and privates wore it on the left sleeves of their coats. General Kearny was killed soon afterward, but veterans of his division still wore the red diamond in his memory.

After General Hooker took command of the Army of the Potomac, he improved on Kearny's original notion. The First Corps had a circle or disk, the Second Corps a three-leaf clover, the Third the diamond. The Fifth wore the Maltese cross. The Sixth Corps had the Greek, or ordinary, cross, like the present-day Red Cross badge. The Eleventh wore a crescent moon; the Twelfth Corps a star.

In every case the three divisions of each corps could be easily seen, too, for the badge or patch of the First Division would be of red, the Second white, the Third blue.

Now let us forget all the other badges except the queer little crescent of the Eleventh Corps. It is sad to remark that, in the Union army during this summer of 1863, the crescent was often looked on as a badge of shame. It was the Eleventh Corps who first gave way at Chancellorsville in May, when they were struck on their flank by the jubilant foot cavalry of Stonewall Jackson.

They went rushing in panic through the woods, and one cannot blame them very much. Few soldiers could survive an attack at one side when they were already being attacked by other troops at their front. It is bad enough to be shot at, but to be shot at from two directions at the same time would break the spirit of practically any man. The Eleventh Corps just happened to be unfortunate at Chancellorsville; now they were equally unfortunate at Gettysburg.

Our Nation in those days was made up more solidly of original English-Irish-Scottish stock than it is now. Great immigrations have taken place through the past century. Today anyone named Kobitsky or Immordino or Patroupolis is just as fine an American as one named Clark, Grant, or Lee. But "furriners" were rather a novelty in 1863, and they were regarded with suspicion. A great many "furriners" were in the

Eleventh Corps; perhaps the majority of these were Germans. The voice speaking in broken English or with a strong accent—was that to be sneered at by people who proudly assumed that they were made of better stuff? A narrow-minded and silly attitude, to be sure . . . wise Americans are still being asked to fight such ignorance today.

Poor Eleventh Corps! Fresh Confederate forces swooped from the northeast, and once more the men with the crescent badge were put to flight. Orders came to retreat. A new attack whirled toward them. In no time at all they were running, fleeing through the village with exultant Rebels hot on their heels.

Out toward the west, on Oak Ridge, which the Federal First Corps still defended, men turned their glasses toward the right flank and saw what had happened. Retreat, retirement, nothing but retreat. So the First Corps had to retreat and stampede into the village from the west, as the Eleventh had done from the north; or they would have been surrounded.

Later there were attempts to deny the speed of this flight. Some of the officers who commanded the Federal troops hated to admit how badly they were whipped.

General Abner Doubleday, who took command of the First Corps after Reynolds was killed, declared: "I waited until the artillery had gone, and then rode back to the town with my staff." He claimed that the First Corps "was broken and defeated, but not dismayed. There were but few left, but they showed the true spirit of soldiers. They walked leisurely from the seminary to the town, and did not run."

On the other hand, Captain Beecham of the Iron Brigade said that his comrades "did not wait a second . . . but dashed down the Chambersburg Pike." He recounted that retiring batteries of artillery "passed us, their horses on a full run, and the cannoneers clinging . . . but we saw nothing of General Doubleday and his staff." It seems that the Union troops ran as fast as they could run.

When the author of this book was young, he talked with many veterans of Gettysburg, and they all told the same story. As the line collapsed north of town, the troops raced down the streets, across yards. They climbed over fences; they ran against clotheslines; they scrambled around woodsheds and dog kennels. They stumbled over cabbage beds in the gardens—slipped and fell among the rhubarb, got up again. Perhaps they fired another shot at the Rebels coming behind them, and then raced for the welcome safety of the cemetery hill. It was rocky up there, with walls and fences: a good place for a defeated army to gather and try to take a new position.

Under the smoky sun of late afternoon, many boys lay motionless where the lines had clashed. They would never rise and run; they would never breathe again. Hundreds of others moaned among torn bushes and ditches of Seminary Ridge, or crawled miserably across little farms north of the village. Others lay, unable to crawl, begging the mad sun to stop its heat, begging for water, with no one to get them any.

Less terrible was the plight of the two or three thousand men who were already captives of the Rebels, though many of these would die later in prison pens. The bulk of them were caught during that wild scramble through the village. They did not know which way the streets ran. They did not know which road leading from the Diamond might take them to safety and which might take them into the very jaws of the pursuing enemy.

East and a little south of the cemetery, separated by a brief valley, rose another cluster of trees and rocks called Culp's Hill. On Culp's Hill the momentarily defeated Union army fastened its right flank, and soon the line of defense was bent in a tight half-circle. North, west, and along the ridge south of the cemetery, survivors of the First and Eleventh Corps worked frantically, building breastworks, trying to fortify themselves against further attack. They tore down fences, moved posts and gates; they rolled stones into place and posted their sharpshooters behind old walls.

Soon after the retreat to Granite Ridge (hereafter called Cemetery Ridge, as it is known today) the Twelfth Corps, under General Slocum, came panting up the Baltimore Pike. They had made a forced march that day from Littlestown. The exhausted Yankees were glad to see reinforcements. They hoped that the other four corps of the Army of the Potomac were hurrying to help them too. The Third Corps, commanded by General Dan Sickles, arrived that same night.

For all practical purposes, General Lee had won the battle of Gettysburg on this Wednesday afternoon of July 1. Yet for some reason he did not order a further attack against the Federal line. People who have spent years in studying the battle have wondered about it. Many say that Robert E. Lee made here the greatest mistake of his career: that this July 1 at Gettysburg was the turning point in Confederate fortunes; that from this hour on, the bright star of Southern secession began to fade. Others defend Lee, and insist that he made a wise choice.

Pretend we are up in a helicopter, high above Gettysburg, with every opportunity to study the situation through powerful field glasses, through the clear understanding of many years.

Thousands of Yankees have been wounded, slain, or captured. The troops who escaped have run pell-mell through the town and are trying to fortify themselves on Cemetery Ridge. From northeast, north, northwest, and west, triumphant Confederates have forced their way across hard-fought land into Gettysburg itself. They too have lost many people during the first day's battle; but in troops already on the scene they have the Yankees vastly outnumbered.

There is the matter of morale, also—the spirit of folks who fight. Men who have been compelled to make a retreat, especially a disorderly one, are apt to continue their retreat if they are pressed firmly from behind. Men who are winning are apt to keep on winning. The sense of victory seems to put fresh life in their bodies, fresh air in their lungs. The Confederates had the most men; they were winning; but no definite orders came for them to charge the slopes of Cemetery Hill or to sweep around behind the Federals' position and cut them off from reinforcement.

General Lee did send a message to Ewell, the one-legged officer who commanded his Second Corps, now at the left of the Confederate line. Lee suggested or advised that Ewell attack the Yankees in their new position if Ewell thought it wise to do so. This was not an order; it could be called a hint.

Ewell did not respond. A few of his soldiers made a feeble movement against the Union right, but when they were met immediately with artillery fire they edged back into town.

Many historians believe that the Northern force present at Gettysburg in that hour was not capable of beating off a heavy attack. Certainly the Rebels were hot and tired, but so were the troops of the Union's Twelfth Corps, now beginning to reach the ridge. Even with the presence of the Twelfth Corps the Yankees had fewer men than the Secessionists. Had the Federal forces been driven away from that strong, rocky ridge, they might have streamed, again disorganized, over regions where there was no such natural opportunity to make a good defense. Thousands more would doubtless have been captured or scattered to the winds.

On the other hand, General Longstreet, commander of Lee's First Corps, did not believe that Lee should have attacked Cemetery Ridge then or even the next day. He wanted Lee to forget all about the Yankees packed along those hills, waiting to resist. He wanted Lee to ignore them, to pass to the south where the other corps were still separated by many miles from each other, and strike toward the city of Washington itself.

Lee did not agree. He said only, "If the enemy is still in that position tomorrow, I shall attack him." But before Lee was ready to give battle on Thursday, July 2, both the Union Second and Third Corps had arrived, and the Fifth and Sixth were coming close. Artillery and ammunition had been brought up in greater quantities.

We look down from our wise height of a later century, and it all seems very simple to us. We would have attacked the hill that very night. We would have crushed these smaller numbers of troops, had we been in the Confederate commander's shoes. It is easy for us to see how cleverly we would have commanded.

Robert E. Lee, examining Cemetery Ridge through his glasses, could not be so sure. The Northern position looked strong. His troops had suffered serious losses. He did not want Ewell's divisions to face a further murderous fire from the rocky walls if Ewell himself did not think it the thing to do.

There had been no time to make a count. Lee did not know, actually, how many of the Yankees had been killed, wounded, and captured by his tired men in gray. He would wait for tomorrow. He would not have such a good chance again, but how did he know?

Not all the soldiers captured during that blazing day had been Federals, especially during the first hours of the fight. General James J. Archer, at the head of a spirited Southern brigade, pressed too eagerly on the Union left and was separated from other brigades near at hand. He and a large portion of his men were quickly surrounded and forced to surrender. As in the case of all captured soldiers, their weapons were taken from them and they were escorted by guards to the rear. There they would not be in the way, and would have no opportunity to assist their comrades during any further attack.

Big, dark-faced General Doubleday rode forward to see who had been captured. He stared, astonished. Here was James Archer, an old classmate of his. Twenty-odd years before, they had been boys in the same class at West Point—good pals during their cadet years, even though they were military enemies now.

"Why, Archer," said Doubleday, extending his hand cordially, "I'm glad to see you!"

General Archer must have been one of the most honest men in the war. He didn't like being captured; nobody does.

"Well, Ab," he cried at Doubleday, "I'm not glad to see *you*. Not by a long sight!"

6

"GET IN THAT HOLE!"

South of the Federal lines stood the Round Tops, high and rocky hills. Even today that would be a good spot to set up some cannon, if people were getting ready for a battle. Gunners would have a clear view of the region all around. Surely, if the Rebels had seized Round Top on July 2, 1863, they could have planted artillery up there and blown the Yankees apart.

War is a mix-up of mistakes, delays, neglect, sudden decisions, sudden attacks, sudden defenses. And luck plays a great part. The Confederate luck seemed to be running out when the battle reopened on Thursday afternoon, July 2.

Rebel commanders thought that they could move far to the south without being seen and then launch a quick overwhelming attack toward Sherfy's peach orchard and a wheat field where

General Dan Sickles had established his Third Corps. But Yankee signal flags were fluttering on Round Top. A handful of blue soldiers hovered there, watching the enemy and wigwagging, by code, any news of Confederate activity. (There were no field telephones, no walkie-talkies at Gettysburg.)

A few disabled soldiers in Federal uniforms, toiling across a field, fell into the hands of the enemy. The Secessionists questioned them closely. These men said that they had been told to report to the surgeon; they thought that they were wandering toward their own rear. Probably they were frightened to death; at any rate they talked, and talked freely.

Round Top, they said, was not held by Union artillery. It was not defended by any worthwhile force at all: only the few signal men. Confederate officers were jubilant when they heard this. They wanted to attack the hills at once—they could haul artillery up and blast the Federal lines from one end to the other.

But no. Their orders were to hit Sickles at the front, not to swing around to the south and right. Desperately the Confederate brigade commanders appealed to General John B. Hood, but he had his orders; he dared not attempt anything contrary.

Hood tried to send a message to General Lee,

telling the Commander in Chief this exciting news: the hills at the Yankee left were undefended. Nobody knows what happened to the messengers, but probably the news never reached Lee's headquarters.

Quickly another order came back from Longstreet, commanding the First Corps. The attack should take place at once. It was late afternoon by this time. The day had been spent in fruitless marching and countermarching. Union forces bristled along the ridges. Time was running out.

Whooping, firing, the Confederates hurled themselves against the angle of the Yankee line formed by Sickles's Third Corps. Artillery had been posted near the Emmitsburg Road. The gray-colored columns were ripped by close-range fire, but the holes closed up. On the gray throngs came, battering Sickles on right and left. The Yankees gave ground at the wheat field and peach orchard.

Some units were being pounded by terrible cross fire; masses of Confederates assailed them on west and south. An urgent message reached General Winfield Hancock: bleeding and exhausted men of the Third Corps cried for aid from their brothers in the Second. Hancock sent a division commanded by General John C. Caldwell.

Hastily every man tightened his belt, examined his cartridge pouch, looked to the loading of his gun. But a strange hush had fallen over the second brigade; others nearby looked bewildered at the scene.

On a boulder stood Father William Corby, the chaplain. Father Corby, a Catholic priest, was there because—almost to a man—the people of this second brigade were Irish Catholics. You look through the rolls now and you find names that make you think of shamrocks and St. Patrick's Day.

O'Brien, Kelly, Harrity, Touhy, Maroney, Burke: a thousand more. They carried, besides the Stars and Stripes, a green flag in memory of the small green island from which they or their parents or grandparents had come. These boys were lions in any fight, but they were devout in their faith. It seemed to the chaplain that they needed a prayer now.

Word of the slaughter on the left had reached this portion of the army. The soldiers knew that they were bound for no picnic, no exciting holiday of storied strife; they were going to wade into the most merciless sort of fighting.

In the Catholic religion there is a ceremony known as absolution. A man confesses his sins, asks God for forgiveness, and finds it. If a person receives absolution when he is about to meet death, his spirit is not troubled as he dies.

But how to forgive so many men who must have had, for all their fitness as soldiers, many sins among them; how might a priest know who was to die, who was to live? Father Corby did not know, but he felt in his tender heart a great love for these rough men. They were his children. He prayed that the Father and Son would look down and approve what he was about to do.

It was the custom to do this, in many European countries: to give absolution, a sincere forgiveness to all troops about to enter battle. Such a ceremony had never been performed in the United States before.

Standing high on that boulder, the air torn by the snarl of red-hot missiles, the priest addressed the brigade. Absolution ... he would give it. If each man sincerely begged for forgiveness and promised, if he lived, to confess his sins in the manner ordered by the Church at the first opportunity, there could be no wrong in performing this ceremony.

Urgently his voice went out. He cried to them to do their duty well. He reminded them that the Church would refuse Christian burial to any soldier who did not uphold his flag, who weakened and ran away. Father Corby lifted his hand. All over that hillside the men began to kneel.

Hot they were beneath the stare of the afternoon sun; they could smell the powder smoke.

The firing on the left, where they were to go, increased to a solid growl. In Latin the priest pronounced the words . . . *"nomine Patris, et Filii, et Spiritus Sancti. Amen."*

This was the last prayer many would ever hear; they would have no ears for hearing in another half-hour. The green flag was carried to the left. The five regiments of the Irish Brigade took their places in the line and took the bullets which were meant for them.

But if you go to Gettysburg today you may see Father Corby there. He is made of bronze. He stands upon that same rock, lifting his hand as he seeks forgiveness for the brave men. Sometimes it almost seems that you can see the brigade kneeling close.

High on an open shelf of Little Round Top stood an officer with a field glass in his hand. His blue uniform was dusty. Dust covered the twin stars of a major general on his shoulders, for Gouveneur K. Warren had been riding far that day. He was chief engineer of the Army of the Potomac. His job was to examine the ground on which fighting might take place.

Peaks, ravines, watercourses, roads: these things Warren knew, and he may have wondered long as he stood, with the noise of the struggle yowling up through the smoke. He may have wondered why General Meade had not seen fit to defend these small mountains.

Suddenly Warren was tense. He bent forward, planting binoculars against his eye sockets. The haze drifted aside. Here was a new piece of luck for the Yankees, a new piece of bad luck for their foe. If Warren had not happened to observe properly, if the smoke had not been twisted by the July wind, there might have been a different story to tell at Gettysburg.

A force of Confederates was sweeping east from the gaunt rocks of Devil's Den, heading directly toward the hill on which Warren stood. In another few minutes this high position would be in the grip of valiant men from Texas and Alabama who had swept over the Yankee resistance. They had not been allowed to attack Round Top earlier, but now they had pushed the blue lines aside. Nothing stood in their way except the rugged slopes of the hills themselves.

General Warren jumped from the boulder and sped away through the trees. His horse was there; his toe found the stirrup. He swung into the saddle; his horse went slipping across uneven ground to the east. Warren broke loose from the green trees. Dust, dust, and the mutter of a hasty marching column. Troops were coming up the Taneytown Road.

What about the signal flags, what about the

wigwag? A message could have been waved to headquarters on Cemetery Hill in a few seconds, but what good would that do? Even if those distant commanders could spare more troops, it was over two miles from the cemetery to Round Top. The nearer Confederates would have seized the hills long before any Yankee regiments could travel that distance.

But the Fifth Corps, Meade's old corps, now commanded by General Sykes—here they were. Stringing along the road, they had marched all day; they were only now reaching the field.

Warren galloped toward them and beckoned breathlessly to mounted officers. That hill behind him . . . Rebs . . . hurry, hurry! . . . A brigade scooted across the fields and labored up the east face of Little Round Top.

This was a mixed brigade: a regiment from Maine, one from New York (Warren's own state), a regiment from Pennsylvania, one from Michigan. Colonel Strong Vincent was the brigade commander, and now he was breathing his last few moments of life. The men who were to kill him and many of his soldiers were Alabamans, clambering up the west side of the hill just as furiously as the Yankees climbed the east.

They met at the summit. Individual rifles began to bang; there was a ragged volley. In another minute all the guns were emptied on both sides and there was no time to reload. Officers fired their revolvers. The men met and wrestled, choking, slugging, rolling off the jagged pinnacles of rock, kicking, hurling stones.

In a few nervous minutes these Yankees had been plucked from the tiresome drudgery of a march and were battling, fist and rifle butt, tooth and claw. In a few shocking minutes the Alabamans, who had won their way through perils of the wheat field and the rocks of Devil's Den, had sprung ardently up a hill where they expected to meet no resistance. They found instead the sweaty men of the Fifth Corps.

Luck again. Never had a force arrived more in the nick of time than had Sykes's corps of Federal troops.

Texans and men from Arkansas hurried to help the other Rebels. Part of a Union brigade commanded by General Stephen Weed came shooting through the trees. The crest of the hill was taken and retaken, but finally, inch by inch, cranny by cranny, the Secesh were driven down the slope. They left the gullies lined with their own dead. They left many blue-clad Yankees there too. Night would find the Round Tops still held by Northerners.

The years to come would bring another unmoving figure to the scene. Like Father Corby, General Warren stands made of metal today, keeping his lonely vigil on that hill.

In the horrid, smoky sunset more troops were locked together than had yet fought during the entire two days. The Federal line was at another moment of peril. Hand-to-hand fighting raged savage and intense near Devil's Den, near the wheat field, on slopes of the Round Tops. Toward the north the constant slam of Confederate fire held the Yankees of the right wing grimly to their task.

There had been gaps in the blue line from time to time that day. Now appeared another empty space, and General A. P. Hill decided to press his advantage. He might even be able to split the Federals near their left center if he acted quickly, before darkness came down.

Hill selected a brigade: Georgians, all of them— four regiments commanded by General Ambrose R. Wright. He hurled them forward under the glare of the low sun.

In dread the Union General Hancock sat his horse on the slope of Cemetery Ridge. He watched the Georgians trotting across the Emmitsburg Road, over broken fences and walls, directed like a bristling arrow against the big gap sagging at Sickles's right.

Hancock slammed his glasses back into their case and gazed about desperately for some means to stop this advance. Who was nearest to the gap? One regiment, the 1st Minnesota Infantry—the only regiment from west of the Mississippi to be engaged in that battle on the Yankee side.

Do you remember the difference in numbers in a Southern brigade and a Northern brigade, a Southern regiment and a Northern regiment? The 1st Minnesota was one of those skeleton regiments. They had fought in other campaigns; the numbers had been reduced by wounds, by death, and sickness. There were two hundred sixty-two now, officers and men; when they had marched away to war there had been over twelve hundred.

But not even then had they strode in numbers to match the strength of these Georgians, veteran troops who came howling across trampled fields, their pinkish flags bobbing. Ragged, hairy men they were, but as capable soldiers as ever came from below the Savannah River.

One little regiment in front of them: two hundred sixty-two.

Hancock is said to have cried to the Minnesota commander, Colonel William Colvill, "Do you see those flags? Take them!" He may or may not have said that. More likely he yelled, "Get in there and stop those Rebs!"

The Minnesotans moved. They went crouching, taking cover behind low boulders as the Sioux Indians (against whom the elder of these men had sometimes fought in Minnesota) might have done. They yelled as the advancing Rebels yelled, but their cry was not the long drawn haunting *whoooo* of the Secesh. They gave the war whoop of the Dakota Indians who had roamed Minnesota plains and forests for so long.

The first volley rang out; answering stabs of flame burst from the spearhead of the Rebel advance. Smoke began to blot the positions. Hancock swept his horse's reins against its neck and dug with his spurs. The Fifth Corps must be somewhere near. If Hancock could meet them, as Warren had already done, and detach some troops quickly, he might be able to plug the wound in the Federal defense after the Confederates had swept the frail 1st Minnesota from their path.

He sent orderlies racing. He raced himself. *Find Sykes.* There was no one else to spare from the right or left of the Federal force. *Find Sykes.* Smoke filled the valley like dust in a saucer. The Sherfy house was blotted out; the Codori farm was covered; you could scarcely see disordered fences or rocks.

Men who watched from other positions heard the yelling, heard the increased spasm of muskets. Now and then they saw the cone of a battle flag upheld. It seemed but a question of minutes before Wright's Rebel brigade would force itself up the slope. Hancock prayed that he could find the Fifth Corps in time.

They were found, uniforms soggy with sweat,

their faces caked, their canteens empty; but their cartridge pouches were full. "Get in that hole," Winfield Hancock cried. "Stop those Rebs. Get in that hole!"

Slowly the yellowish smoke went up; the haze thinned. No Confederates climbed the low crest; no banners bearing the St. Andrew's cross were planted amid the rocks. A brigade from Sykes's corps went panting down the fields.

They began to stumble over objects lying in their path. Flat rolls . . . like logs . . . rocks around them were splotched with the black spittle of leaden bullets. Here was the 1st Minnesota indeed, all two hundred sixty-two of them. Only thirty-seven were still able to fire and run and shriek defiance at the four regiments they had halted in that trampled grass. Two hundred twenty-five boys and men lay bleeding among weeds and boulders. They had plugged the hole in the Union line before fresh troops ever reached the scene.

It is often presumed that the Confederates were outnumbered in most battles during the Civil War. Many times they were; often the Rebels fought as bravely against overwhelming odds as any Americans ever fought—as any men of any nation ever fought any time, any place.

But on July 2, 1863, amid the jimson weeds and scattered granite of a single farm, the 1st

Minnesota balked a striking force of Southerners outnumbering them eight to one.

Colonel Colvill had been wounded during the first few minutes; Captain Messick took command. Soon he was killed. Captain Farell then took command. He fell bleeding. Captain Muller was next. He was wounded soon, so Captain Periam commanded the regiment until a bullet found him. When this bitter fight ended, Captain Henry C. Coates was at the head of the survivors—the sixth officer to succeed in command. The regiment lost 86 percent of its number in fifteen minutes. Such a thing had never happened elsewhere in our history except during an Indian massacre.

7

COLD WATER, COLD WATER

A coppery sunset glared hard in the eyes of Union soldiers as they aimed toward the west; but the sun was behind Rebel sharpshooters who crouched amid the cavelike holes of Devil's Den. That same sunset made the shapes of Yankees stand out easily on the Round Tops. They were like toy figures in a shooting gallery.

Though the Southern army lacked much in the way of equipment, the powder in their cartridges was better than the Yankee ammunition. It was brought from Europe by sly sea captains who guided blockade-running vessels past Northern fleets guarding all the Southern ports. Many ships slid regularly in and out, under cover of darkness and fog. On their return voyages they brought the finest gunpowder which French and English arsenals could sell.

The Northern powder was made at home by contractors working for the government. Many of the contractors were cheats and swindlers. They used too much charcoal—which was cheap. Worse than that, some of them padded the powder with nothing more or less than black dirt. The Northern cartridges misfired often, and when the explosion did occur, a soldier could not be sure that his bullet would travel all the distance it was supposed to go.

Stories were told about Yankees who took great risks to prowl close to the Rebel positions and steal some of the better powder from pouches of the dead Confederates. The Southern sharpshooters had a double advantage at sunset on July 2: better ammunition, better light to shoot by.

As individual Yankee artillerymen leaped forward to manage their cannon they fell before the accurate aim of the gray sharpshooters. Sometimes every man of a gun crew was killed or wounded in rapid succession.

An entire battery of U.S. regular artillery had been hauled to the summit of Little Round Top. Men dragged ropes, men grasped and shoved with the strength of their shoulders, to force the dead weight of the cannon upward.

This battery was commanded by Lieutenant Charles E. Hazlett. It had been moved up to support the defense by General Stephen Weed's brigade. Weed was instructing Hazlett about where he wanted the battery to fire . . . a bullet whined and struck. General Weed sprawled across the stones.

Hazlett bent over him. Weed was still trying to talk, trying to give him an urgent command with his last strength. Another bullet moaned. Hazlett fell dead across Weed's body.

It seemed like committing suicide to try to fire those cannon. Yet other men came forward to do it, and at last the shiny weapons began to blast against the fatal rocks of Devil's Den, where marksmen were concealed. Shells burst like awful blossoms in the dusk. Thus a grim miracle came about.

After the battle Confederate boys would be found high amid the stony gashes, guarding the gnarly hill in death as they had held it in life. They would have no marks on their bodies; but still they would be dead. Killed—by the very concussion of shells smashing amid those immovable rocks. Killed—by crushing air which sped out like lightning to slay them, even when the fragments of metal did not touch.

With darkness the fighting ended at the Confederate right. The Union Third Corps had been pressed back from its exposed position. The Rebels held Devil's Den, the peach orchard, the region along the Emmitsburg Road. But they had failed in their attempt to seize the heights beyond.

A ruddy moon came up—yellow later, whitish-green at last—to gleam on the wreckage of the second day. Occasionally a sentry thought he saw enemies creeping close....He fired. There rattled a brief exchange of shots, little jabs of flame in the moonlight. Then silence, except for the eternal wail of wounded men.

In the dusk, as the fire slackened south of town, the hollow of Middle Street in Gettysburg was filled with quiet armed men. They moved stealthily along a lane northeast of Cemetery Hill. They didn't smoke for fear the Yankees would see the glow of pipes. When they whispered to one another, many of them spoke in French.

These were the Louisiana Tigers, one of the prize brigades in the Southern army. They were made up mostly of men of French ancestry, as many Louisiana people are descended from the French. The Tigers had other troops to support them.

In early evening they crept silently toward the walls which rimmed the cemetery. The fight was short but bitter. The Federals had mounted guns on Culp's Hill, and there were cannon in the cemetery itself. For a time it was another hand-to-hand struggle. Cannoneers fought with their ramrods when gray men came whooping among them. Rocks were hurled. People were slugged and choked with bare hands.

Union reinforcements came sprinting across the cemetery, stumbling over graves and tombstones, but rushing on to the wall where the Confederate attack swayed. Under this fresh onset, the Tigers and their supporters gave way. Once removed from the Yankee position, they received the full blast of canister on their front and from Culp's Hill on their left. Nearly a thousand of them lay helpless when the survivors had drifted back to the darkened valley.

Early the next morning another attack was made by the Confederate General Ed Johnson's division, on Culp's Hill itself. This assault was beaten off. Again a Gettysburg hillside was matted with the bodies of those who had tried to take the hill, the bodies of those who had died to defend it.

There were several families of Culps living close; and a young man, Wesley Culp, was a nephew of the owner of that hill. When he was only a boy, Wesley had gone down South to live. It was natural that he grew to have sympathy for the South, because that was where he lived, that was where his friends lived. When the war broke out, Wesley Culp became a soldier in gray instead of a soldier in blue. The sun of Friday, July 3, would recognize him lying on the side of Culp's

Hill. He had come home at last, come from the distant South to die on his uncle's land, near the house where he was born.

The bullets did not respect gold braid. At least one hundred forty generals, North and South, were killed in action or died of wounds during the Civil War. More generals were killed or wounded at Gettysburg alone than you could count on the fingers of your hands and the toes of your feet.

Modern warfare is conducted differently. America lost a number of fine leaders during World War II and in Korea but, speaking as a whole, commanders nowadays do not rush madly to the front in every encounter. We do not want them to. The Nation has spent years of time, thousands and thousands of dollars, in training a man for leadership. The Nation has much invested in him; he would be difficult to replace.

In the forefront of attack, a general represents nowadays only one more finger on a trigger, only one more hand on the controls of a tank or an aircraft. Back in his post of command he is a guiding genius, instantly ready to give advice or orders by radio or telephone. His presence in this post of command may save hundreds of other lives.

But at Gettysburg it was considered proper for

generals to lead their brigades in person. The worst feature of it was that customarily senior officers were mounted on horseback, whereas the men marched on foot. The commanders presented easy targets to a watching foe—proud men on their horses, high above the mass.

Through the tawny smoke of July 2, a brigade of Mississippians had come yelling, urged on by General William Barksdale. The Yankee lead poured thick, the Mississippi lines were torn, survivors closed up the gaps: on they charged. Barksdale was a hearty man with a loud voice and an impressive appearance. He had served his country in Congress before the war; now he served his State just as energetically.

He was dressed in a short gray jacket and gray trousers; on his head he wore a red fez, such as Muslims wear in the Eastern nations. Barksdale rode closer and closer to the Northern line, waving his sword, bellowing encouragement to his men. He may have thought they could not go on without him.

Captain Ira W. Cory of the 11th New Jersey bit his lip. This one eager man, with his red fez and his sword, was a model for the rest. He was worth a whole regiment of ordinary folks; he must be brought down at all costs. An aide had just galloped up, bringing a grim order which the captain had to obey.

Captain Cory snapped a command. The whole

of Company H turned their rifles toward Barksdale. "That big Reb," said the captain. "Get him." The fatal volley rapped, the sturdy figure toppled, the scarlet cap was seen no more.

Hours later, through moonlight and shadow, a young man named Joseph Muffly limped into a farmyard behind the Federal lines. Muffly, serving as adjutant of the 148th Pennsylvania, had been hit in the leg during the afternoon. Perhaps he was looking for medical attention.

All around him rose the whine of wounded men; shrieks came from within the house. This had been the home of the Jacob Hummelbough family. Surgeons had taken possession to make a field hospital there. All through the night they were operating. Groaning victims filled the barn and the yard around it. The same was true of a dozen other farms in the Gettysburg neighborhood.

Joseph Muffly heard a deep commanding voice rising above the ugly sounds.

"Cold water, cold water," the voice was saying. "Yes, yes! I want cold water. When I am well, I am a great lover of water—" There was the laughter of delirium.

On a stretcher in the yard lay the shattered body of General Barksdale. With the decency of their kind, the surgeons had tried to undo the harm which weapons of their comrades had caused. The big Mississippian's body had been fairly sieved by Yankee bullets. His breast was so badly torn that one surgeon believed the general had been wounded by grapeshot from a cannon, instead of spiteful little musket balls. His left leg was almost in pieces.

Beside him knelt a thin little drummer boy. The boy had a can of water and he was giving the dying general sips from a spoon he held.

"Cold water," Barksdale gasped. "Now, when I am all shot to pieces—I'm burning with fever—I must have cold water—"

In saner moments he asked how strong the Union army was; men told him that heavy reinforcements were coming. He jeered, "Militiamen?" He cried, "Just you wait until morning! General Lee will show you a trick or two. Yes, yes, you think you have whipped us, but wait until morning, and you will hear Ewell thundering in your rear!"

Before daylight Barksdale had gone to join all the staunch American generals of the past, who waited in Eternity for their battle-torn comrades of the future. The surgeon who attended him wrote down a description of Barksdale's clothing so that there would be no mistake: these details would be published in the press, and the hero's friends would know for a certainty that their general had died within the Yankee lines. The description mentions a "fine linen or cotton shirt which was closed by three studs bearing Masonic emblems."

This suggests the great part borne in the war by members of the Masonic Lodge. Brothers of this organization understood that their first duty was to their armies; the ties of Freemasonry were not more important than their individual loyalties to the Union or Confederate causes. But once a man had been struck and lay helpless, he might expect an especial tenderness from others who held his belief.

It is difficult to imagine a devout Catholic who, finding a wounded enemy with a tiny cross around his neck or a rosary clutched in his hand, would not help this fellow who had lately sought to kill him and whom he had tried to kill.

Amid the worst fighting at Gettysburg a middle-aged Southern general sprang over a wall and leaped fairly amid the Northern cannon. He screamed a last command to his men—"Give 'em the cold steel, boys!" and then he was hit.

A little later, when the Rebels had been driven back, two Federal officers knelt beside the bleeding Confederate.

"Shall we take him to the surgeon at once?" asked one.

The other nodded. "Yes, didn't you hear him? He has called for help—" He whispered the secret words which indicated to these Northern Masons that their brother from the South had given a call for assistance which was centuries old.

Contrary to the dying Barksdale's prophecy, the only thundering which Ewell did in the Yankee rear in the early morning of July 3 was the fruitless assault of Johnson's division on the slopes of Culp's Hill.

Jeb Stuart's cavalry, long absent on a raid around the entire Yankee army, had at last joined Lee's command. Lee sent Stuart to the north and east, past the Union right. He was to try to busy the enemy in that direction while Lee prepared for a grand attack against Cemetery Ridge. In other words, Stuart was to create a "diversion," a strategy by which a leader diverts part of his strength to strike the enemy at a point where his main blow is not intended to fall.

Stuart's diversion did not work out as Lee expected or hoped. The gray troopers were exhausted from days of hard riding; so were their horses. At a crossroad a few miles east of Gettysburg they encountered the cavalry of a Federal general named David Gregg. With him was a younger, jauntier general in blue whose name would later become famous from his fighting in the Indian wars—George A. Custer.

Stuart's weary Confederates were no match for this fresh force. The Yankees had had days of rest, good food; their weapons were ready, so was the spirit of the men. Stuart owned a record of many successful battles against the cavalry of the North, but he could not add to his list of triumphs now. When the last clattering charge had echoed back across this sunny farmland, Stuart's cavalry was in full retreat. General Wade Hampton, one of the most active Southern leaders, was nursing a saber cut on his head.

The Northern leader, General Meade, was not fooled by this rush of cavalry behind his main position, nor were his men. They expected that the most ferocious attack would come from the west, swinging against the center and left of the Union line. That was where it came.

But not until afternoon. Lee wanted to pave the way with a terrific artillery bombardment. He had to spend hours getting his guns into position.

There was some mild activity near the cemetery. The barn on the Bliss farm was filled with Secesh marksmen, and they were giving the Unionists along the ridge a bad time. At length they were driven out and the barn was burned.

The Union soldiers behind the sloping stone walls settled down to wait. More than a mile away, beyond the Emmitsburg Road and along its lower portions, they could see the enemy guns trundling about. "It'll be hot," they muttered to one another.

8

"I SHALL GO FORWARD, SIR"

The cannon of Civil War times were nothing like the fast-recoiling tubes used today on tanks and half-tracks. They were stubby; some were made of brass, some of bronze, some of wrought iron. The barrels balanced between two wheels, with a sloping tail called a prolonge.

Some of the muzzles showed the marks of rifling: little ridges within the bore, to direct the shell upon its way, as a bullet whirls out of a .22 rifle. These were for long range. A mile was considered quite a long range, in that war.

Other batteries had smoothbore cannon. There were brass guns called Napoleons, and fat howitzers. The purpose of these weapons was to fire at troops when they came close. Powder would be put into the barrel, then bags of small balls (or big round cannonballs). Sometimes cannon were stuffed full of scrap metal—old rusty nails, anything which could be blasted forth and thus kill the approaching enemies.

Usually a battery was made up of six cannon. There were dozens of batteries in the artillery brigades of both armies at Gettysburg. The boys who served as cannoneers had to stuff ammunition into the weapons from the front end. They would use ramrods; powder and shot would be jammed in, the cannon would be fired by a little cap flashing through its touchhole at the breech.

A swab was plunged into a bucket of water and wiped hurriedly all the way through the gun's barrel, to put out any burning sparks clinging inside. Then more powder and shot, another cap; so it would go.

In all the batteries, North and South, at Gettysburg, there were only two guns which might be called modern. These were Whitworth cannon; a recent invention, they had been shipped by the Confederates from England. Like weapons of today, these guns had doors at the breeches; ammunition was put in from the rear.

The projectile fired by a Whitworth gun was called a bolt, and made a strange whirring sound as it flew. It could travel several miles with accuracy—much farther than the other cannon could shoot.

These Whitworths would give a signal for opening the attack.

General George E. Pickett was to act as right guide of the Rebel advance. His division, in Longstreet's First Corps, had not previously fought at Gettysburg. They had been left behind, guarding trains and supplies at Chambersburg. Here they were now: three fresh brigades commanded by Generals Garnett, Kemper, and Armistead. The men seemed competent as they waited in the shade along Seminary Ridge.

But older and more experienced soldiers murmured suspiciously as they gazed toward the Yankee lines. They saw that the Confederate troops would have to cross a wide, flat valley before they reached the enemy. All the way they could be pounded by the Yankee cannon. At one point the Confederate columns were about a mile and a quarter from the enemy lines, at the nearest perhaps three quarters of a mile away. The midday sun broiled down.

Pickett commanded five or six thousand Confederate men in his three brigades. On his left were men of Heth's and Pender's divisions. Heth and Pender had been wounded; Generals Pettigrew and Trimble were now in command of their men. Other brigades stood ready to support. There were about ten thousand soldiers waiting to form this left-side portion of the advance.

In both armies the infantry crouched silently, wondering what was in store. The artillery stood in position. For years afterward men spoke in awe of the strange, wide hush which had fallen over the region. Far off in haze sounded the faint turning of wheels, the neigh of horses—even a queer rooster cry rising from perplexed chickens still scratching about on some war-muddled farm. But a hundred and fifty thousand men scarcely spoke, scarcely breathed.

At one o'clock there was a bright flash from the little Whitworth battery, closely followed by another. Two bolts from the signal guns tore high above the heads of the Rebels, on across the Emmitsburg Road. They descended, hissing.

Where Hancock's Second Corps knelt and watched, a party of high-ranking Union officers had gathered to eat a hasty lunch at the invitation of General John Gibbon, commanding the 1st Division of the Second Corps. Gibbon's orderly had served the generals and their staff officers some bread and meat. He turned again; he was just starting to hand out the butter. A Whitworth bolt screamed down and cut the orderly in two.

An earthquake had come to Pennsylvania. Men had made it. They had wheeled one hundred fifty cannon into position on the Confederate side. Opposite them, on Cemetery Ridge and hills to the left, were eighty or ninety Yankee guns.

"Number One, fire! Number Two, fire—" The officers shrieked their orders above the roar. Although the necessary time was taken for swabbing and loading, yet the number of cannon made a solid thunder; the air was never still. The noise rose to a hurricane, drifted lower, broke out with a fresh blast.

All along the middle of the Yankee lines, most especially in those fields where the Second Corps bent beneath the storm, the shell bursts sprayed in silver and gold. Men who watched from ridges far away could not speak; they could only stare and wonder. Veterans of Chancellorsville, Fredericksburg, Manassas, and other battles, they had never seen or heard anything like this. Lee's artillerymen seemed to be pouring out, in gushing flame, every shell, every ounce of powder they had brought along.

In addition to the cannon themselves, the batteries were made up of other wheeled vehicles. There were the limber chests: little carts to be fastened ahead of the cannon prolonges; cannoneers rode upon these chests when the guns were moving. There were caissons too—huge portable cupboards wherein extra ammunition was stored.

Amid the rain of Confederate fire, caissons were blowing up in the Union lines. One officer stood high on top of his caisson; he could direct his cannoneers better from this position. Suddenly there was a splintering flash. People rubbed their eyes. They could not see any caisson at all—only slow-rising smoke, only a hole in the ground and a few fragments of spokes and wheels. That whole chest of ammunition had been exploded as a shell came down; the officer was blown to bits.

Fifteen minutes, half an hour, three quarters—with shaking hands, men opened their old-fashioned watches and stared at the dials. The little hands were crawling into a new hour. Still the roar continued, the shells soared high. Sometimes they met in midair and burst together high above the troops. Usually they found their way to the targets, and more men were blotted out.

Union General Winfield Hancock began to wonder whether flesh and blood could endure such hammering any longer. People tried to hold him back, but Hancock was bound to show himself to his soldiers, to hearten them, to let them know that he was near.

He climbed on his horse—erect, fine-featured, the wind of battle stroking his thick mustache and little goatee. General Hancock rode along his lines while shells still crashed, drumming the ground, spangling his staff with smoke and hot metal. He forced his big horse over the wreckage of limber chests, past the sprawled bodies of boys who would never know what hoofs trod so close.

The living soldiers saw him. They stood up and began to yell. They would let their general know that they were not frightened away from the front lines, that they would be there, ready to hold the Confederates when they came across.

"*Han*cock! *Han*cock!"

They whooped his name, a hundred throats crying it, and then a thousand and another thousand. The big soldier guided his horse through the smoke, waving his hat in his hand.

Over on the Confederate side even General Lee heard the cheering. He did not know what was happening . . . perhaps the Yankees were cheering as they launched an attack before he was ready to launch his. He even sent officers to ride closer to the Yankees, to learn what it was all about.

The reply of the Union batteries had fallen off, and many Confederates believed that the bulk of the enemy guns was silenced for good. But General Hunt, who commanded Meade's artillery, had stopped some of his guns for a good purpose. They were the rifled cannon mentioned earlier. They were not good for close-range work. Hunt was having his artillerymen cut the dead horses loose from their harnesses and "limber up"—that is, to fasten the cannon to the limber chests and pull them away. He was replacing them as fast as he could with short-range bronze guns. These could be loaded with grapeshot that would cut advancing troops down in solid heaps as they swarmed near.

Colonel Alexander, who commanded guns on the Confederate right, had hoped to silence the Yankee batteries by this time. He did not want the infantry to advance while they still might be torn to pieces before they ever reached the lines.

The Rebels knew that they must save a good portion of their powder to support the infantry as it charged across the valley. If they kept on casting forth ammunition so lavishly they would have little left.

Alexander sent a note to Pickett: "If you are coming at all you must come at once, or I cannot give you proper support. . . . At least eighteen guns are still firing from the cemetery itself."

About this time, one young cannoneer saw the warning sign that had been put up in the cemetery so long ago:

ALL PERSONS FOUND USING FIREARMS IN
THESE GROUNDS WILL BE PROSECUTED WITH
THE UTMOST VIGOR OF THE LAW.

The sign was still there; one young cannoneer saw it. The rows of guns howled with their burnt throats as the boys pointed. Other Yankee cannoneers saw the sign and they screamed with laughter. They went on working their guns, naked to the waist, their arms and faces smeared black as if they had been playing with tar.

Two hundred thirty-eight heated metal voices ... at least that many were roaring when the bombardment began and through its early moments. No portion of the United States had ever been shaken by such fire. In Baltimore, fifty miles away, people ran from their houses, wondering and fearful. In Washington, sixty miles as the crow flies, women stood in their gardens on the outskirts of the capital city. They looked at the northern sky and guessed whether it was going to rain. In Philadelphia, nearly a hundred miles to the east, it was said that people felt the ground shaking.

Another note sped from Colonel Alexander to George Pickett: "For God's sake, come quick ... or my ammunition won't let me support you properly."

Pickett looked at the note. He handed it to General Longstreet. "General, shall I advance?"

Longstreet could imagine, in anguish, the number of his troops who would end their lives in those smoky fields. He tried to utter a word; he could say nothing. He only bowed his head as if in agreement.

Pickett wore long hair close to his shoulders,

with a little cap over one ear. He saluted his chief. "I shall go forward, sir." He turned his horse.

His brigades followed in perfect order: Garnett, Kemper, Armistead. Garnett, a middle-aged officer with a fine record, was a sick man. He had risen from an ambulance bed to lead his brigade; hot as it was, his invalid's body was chilly; he was buttoned up in a blue overcoat. Perhaps that overcoat was a relic of the days when he had been an officer of the United States Army.

The troops on the left, under Trimble and Pettigrew, pressed in support of Pickett's division. A vast brown-gray sea they were, their musket barrels shining as they stepped, more than fifteen thousand men, from the shelter of woods and headed east across the fields.

Yankee guns began to speak again. Bursts appeared in the ranks; the roses of death bloomed; the troops moved on and out; the sun stared to see them.

It was a death march three quarters of a mile wide. There were as many soldiers as might live in a fair-sized city, forming in front by companies and carrying their guns as if they were marching on parade. They paused once as they came within range to hurl a single volley at the Federals. Then reloading, they advanced, changing direction as their officers wished. The fireworks of shell bursts bit into their ranks.

At the Emmitsburg Road they halted and changed direction once again. Faintly the Yankee skirmishers, spraddled behind rocks and bushes out ahead of their lines, could hear officers crying orders. "Column...left oblique...*ha!*" The generals, the mounted officers of field grade, were toppling from their horses as the Union bullets buzzed to meet them. Garnett fell. His old blue overcoat went down into the tide as he vanished.

In later years a relative of General Pickett wrote a book. In it she declared that Pickett rushed all the way into the Yankee lines, striking furiously with his sword, his long hair blowing. How he escaped death, this relative said, was a miracle.

According to other testimony, Pickett halted in the shelter of a barn on the Codori farm. The French artist, Phillipoteaux, who made a great cyclorama of the battle, painted him so. If the division commander did indeed gallop furiously into the Yankee lines, there is no record among Northern witnesses that he did so. It would have been a foolish thing; his services would have been lost to the South from that day forth.

But his men came on. So did the Tennesseans and Georgians and North Carolinians on the left. There were fifteen regiments from the Tar Heel State alone. Years after the battle the sculptor Gutzon Borglum paid his tribute to the coura-

geous Tarheels of North Carolina. At the point
from which they began their bullet-stung advance, there stands now a gigantic group: soldiers crouching embattled into the pressure of
the years. The legend speaks for itself: one out of
every four men who fell here was a North Caro-
linian.

... They were shrieking their battle cry, the
Rebel Yell. It moaned above the horse screams,
the stammer of Yankee fire, the boom of cannon.
They were running, climbing the slope; many had
clapped their bayonets to the muzzles of empty
rifles. Their orders were to seize that position if
they could; they were going to try.

The point selected for the center of their charge
was a little group of oak trees. They were small
trees then, that clump or copse; they are not
much bigger today; soil is rocky and thin upon
that ridge.

The Federals holding the fence angle beside the
copse had been lashed for nearly two hours by
enemy shells. They were torn again by the blast
of Alexander's batteries, which limbered up and
followed behind the advancing columns, firing
over the heads of the gray swarm. Still the surviving Yankees waited, breathing hard, huddling
close behind the old stone fence with heaps of
rails atop.

Whooping in on the Confederate right flank

came a brigade of Vermonters. One young Union officer was under arrest because of some military rule which he had broken. When an officer was under arrest, he was not allowed to carry side arms. So this youth had been deprived of his sword and revolver. But he led his troops just the same. He had found a hatchet, and he waved this over his head as he charged at the Rebels.

On the left Pettigrew had fallen, Trimble had gone down, most of the other field officers as well. Kemper was wounded; Armistead was the only brigade commander to cross the wall. The others were gone. Armistead took his cap from off his bald head and put it on the point of his sword. He held the cap high as a guide to the few following him. He climbed the wall. Bullets found him at last. He fell beside the gun of a Union battery.

The battery was commanded by a lieutenant named Cushing. Coolly he had directed his fire for an hour and a half, though he was shot through both thighs. Cannoneers lay dead around him. There was only Cushing's hand to pull the little lanyard, the cord which fired the cannon.

Cushing gasped that he would fire one more shot. He had been struck again, this time in the abdomen. With his last strength he jerked the lanyard. The cannon barked briefly between its wheels.

Of the Confederates who penetrated beyond the

stone wall fairly into the Yankee lines, not one returned. The remnants faded away, disordered, exhausted—a mere fraction of those who had crossed the summit of western ridges that afternoon.

The sun fell lower, staring crimson through the smoke. Remnants of Pickett's, Pettigrew's, and Trimble's divisions staggered to safety amid distant trees. A big gray-bearded man on a gray horse came to meet them.

He had tears in his voice and in his eyes. "It was all my fault," Robert E. Lee had the courage to say. "Now let us save what we can."

9

THE LIGHTNING CAME

On the morning of July 3, hours after the dead of the Culp's Hill attack had fallen among the rocks, but hours before the invasion of Confederates struggled across the Emmitsburg Road, a young woman of twenty arose brightly in her home on Baltimore Street in order to serve her sister.

She was Mary Virginia Wade. We may guess how she carried nourishing soup to the proud Georgia, who still lay in bed with her tiny week-old son. The next day would be Georgia's own birthday, as well as the nation's.

Biscuits. Virginia Wade could make good biscuits, and at 8:30 A.M. she stood before a table, her hands busy with dough. Occasional fire of sharpshooters in the town flicked out toward the high Federal lines; answering shots drilled down

Baltimore Street. But by this time Ginny Wade and her sister felt more secure, as did most of Gettysburg.

Cannon had roared, rifles had jabbered; this was the third day, and no citizens had been hurt if they did not poke themselves directly into the battle as John Burns had done. Furthermore the brick house seemed substantial: Minié balls pecked at the village walls, but bricks could stop any ordinary bullet. A wooden door could not.

Ginny had her back toward the closed door of the room. Another door beyond was closed also, but quickly a stray bullet found its way through two panels of wood and into her body. She died, mild-faced, comely, the only Gettysburg civilian to be killed in that battle.

"Jenny" Wade; so the world knows her now. Verses have been written about her, and little books, too, and today the house where she died is a museum. Many people have gone there to see the bullet holes in the doors.

Why do people say "Jenny" Wade when her name was Virginia? That is the way legends grow, and often they are false. Her friends spoke of her in nickname fashion as Gin or Ginny. Thus, after she had been buried out in the garden on the following day, her poor body wrapped in an old pink comforter, some reporter went wandering off to write his story for a distant press. He had heard folks speak of "Ginny"; he thought they said "Jenny"; the tale was repeated all over in papers and magazines. Jenny Wade became a tradition, but wearing the wrong name.

The making of history is a difficult and mixed-up process. False impressions are gained merely because tales have gone wrong in the first telling.

Pickett's charge—you have just read about it; yet still it is commonly believed that General Pickett commanded the entire advance and that all the men who ran, perspired, and died in that fatal, futile attempt were Virginians. Pickett commanded roughly one third of the troops in the charge; two thirds of them were commanded by other men: Pettigrew and Trimble. Many of these other troops were North Carolinians. How did such an error ever become accepted?

Easily enough. The newspapers of Richmond, Virginia, naturally made much of the heroic assault. The Richmond editors were concerned more with deeds of men from their own state than they were with North Carolina people and the rest. Thus they spoke of "Pickett's charge." The Richmond newspapers were among the most famous ones in the South at that time and the only Southern papers which reached the North in any quantity. Northern editors read the Virginia accounts and commented on them.

In later years even a great poet like Stephen

Vincent Benét in his famous *John Brown's Body* would write:

> ... *Stepping like deer,*
> *The Virginians, the fifteen thousand.* ...

Many poems have been written about Gettysburg, and one of the most commonly quoted is that which relates the heroism of old John Burns. The verses were written by Francis Bret Harte. Unfortunately, the poem is filled with as much falsehood and fancy as it is with fact.

> ... *Held his own in the fight next day,*
> *When all his townsfolk ran away.*
> *That was in July, sixty-three,—*
> *The very day that General Lee,*
> *Flower of Southern chivalry,*
> *Baffled and beaten, backward reeled*
> *From a stubborn Meade and a barren field.*

The verse is stirring, but it is nonsense. General Lee's army certainly did not reel backward on that first day at Gettysburg when John Burns fought alongside the Yankees. It was the Yankees who fled—at least those who were not dead or lying wounded, or who were not captured by the Confederates.

"When all his townsfolk ran away." The few

people who had fled from Gettysburg did so at the time of General Early's advance through town a week before. Practically no others had any opportunity to flee even if they wanted to, during the battle. Roads were choked in every direction, crowded with troops, crammed with wagons and cannon and caissons.

It seems that someone might have told Bret Harte how many willing Pennsylvanians were already serving in the armies of the North. Company after company had been raised in that vicinity. The 87th Pennsylvania Infantry, not engaged at Gettysburg but elsewhere, was made up almost entirely of Adams County boys.

So raged the battle. You know the rest:
How the rebels, beaten and backward pressed,
Broke at the final charge and ran.
At which John Burns—a practical man—
Shouldered his rifle, unbent his brows,
And then went back to his bees and cows.

It might have been very convenient for the North if the "rebels, beaten and backward pressed," had indeed broken at the final charge and run away on Wednesday, July 1. They did not.

As for John Burns, he was painfully wounded during the fight and, according to one historian, "fell into the hands of the Confederates and came very near being executed." This was because Burns was not in uniform. He was a citizen, not a soldier; if citizens attempt to fight military enemies, they are apt to be executed. Poor old Burns had to move about on crutches for a long time after the battle, though he did not die until 1872.

These little incidents—the untrue versions and the true versions—are set down for a special purpose. They are not told in order to poke fun at the writers. They are told in order to show the way in which mistaken information can lead to mistakes in history.

History is tangled, history is strange. No two men ever witness the same portions of a battle. Each tells his story the way he saw it or the way he remembers it. Very often a man's honest memory may be at fault. And then you have a hundred ex-soldiers each giving his own tale, or sometimes a thousand. The scholar who would try to separate the true facts from the imaginary story must feel that he is losing his mind.

One writer says a regiment was entrenched at this point. "No," says writer number two, "only a company." "I was there," cries a third voice. "No one built a trench at that place. They built it away over *there*." In after years the students come to peek and poke. They try to find old marks of shoveling, the spent bullets, the bones, the rusty flakes of an army in the soil. Sometimes they cannot find them.

Two days before the battle began, a slim, tall captain had been promoted to the rank of brigadier general by General Alfred Pleasonton, who commanded the entire corps of Union cavalry in the Gettysburg campaign. Nowadays a captain might be promoted to the rank of major for gallantry in the field—captains often are. But in the Civil War it was not unusual for an officer of comparatively low rank to find himself suddenly wearing the stars of a general.

George A. Custer had become a general when the doors of West Point were scarcely closed behind him. Elon J. Farnsworth, in his middle twenties, found himself commanding a brigade. Farnsworth had not yet received his commission. He had only been told that he was promoted. His admirer and commander, General Pleasonton, generously shared his own wardrobe with Farnsworth. He gave the new brigadier one of his own jackets with a single star for insignia, instead of the captain's bars which the young officer had worn before.

Elon Farnsworth's immediate superior was General Judson Kilpatrick. He too was a very young man, a bold soldier who bore not too happy a reputation with his own men. In fact, behind his back they called Kilpatrick "Kill Cavalry."

Kilpatrick sent Farnsworth to the far left of the Union line while the terrible cannonade was still going on. When the firing stopped, when the Rebel advance had been beaten back, Kilpatrick decided that he would try to have his men break through the Secesh brigades that were holding the right of the enemy line before him.

It was rugged country, just west and a little south of Round Top. Devil's Den was toward the north, the Emmitsburg Road toward the west, and in between there lay more boulders, more woods, more rocky little creeks. Rail and stone fences stretched in several directions. It is hard for horses to run at a gallop over ground like this, but Farnsworth did his best.

He rode with his men. They came under a hail of bullets from gray regiments crouching behind the stone walls. Shells from a battery burst among them; boys fell from their saddles. The wounded riderless horses went screaming and hobbling about.

Farnsworth was beaten back and hesitated about making any further attempt. Cavalry could not attack successfully amid boulders and ravines where they met a withering fire poured from natural forts.

He turned to find Kilpatrick riding close.

"I was near Kilpatrick," wrote Captain Parsons of the 1st Vermont Cavalry, "when he . . . gave the order to Farnsworth to make the last charge."

Farnsworth could not believe his ears. He was having his men torn to bits needlessly. Nothing could be gained; General Meade had sent no infantry to support this attempt. Even if the Yankees succeeded in breaking the Rebel line, they could not hold the gains they had made and chew their way through more opposition to cut off Lee's line of retreat—not unless a vast column of infantry moved in to help.

"General, do you mean it?" Elon Farnsworth cried. "Shall I throw my handful of men over rough ground, through timber? . . . These are too good men to kill."

Kilpatrick was furious. "If you're afraid to lead this charge, I'll lead it myself!" he yelled.

The new general stood up in his stirrups, white with rage. He screamed, "Take that back!"

Kilpatrick was ashamed. "I didn't mean that," he said more soothingly to Farnsworth. "Forget it."

But the young officer's pride had been stung. He spoke again, calmly: "I will lead the charge."

Farnsworth took his troops on a wild, hopeless ride over rocks and through gulleys. They left their dead stringing behind. Nowadays a monument tells of this bravery and this sadness: a bas-relief—a sculptured mass of boys and horses, riding forever at full career.

Farnsworth's horse was shot; he jumped to the ground, he took another horse from one of his troopers, he galloped on. He forced his way close to the muzzles of the Rebel guns; they riddled him. General Pleasonton's borrowed blue coat was torn to rags. There were five wounds in Farnsworth's body when men picked him up; any one of those wounds could have been fatal.

Clouds formed around the horizon. A vast thickness of sour smoke drenched the farmlands of long valleys. Bruised, quivering, the survivors of the two armies faced each other on into the dusk.

The Union lines lay very much as they had lain for two days. The Secessionists clung to Seminary Ridge and the areas where they had been clinging before. What had been accomplished? The mowing down of thousands and thousands of Americans who would never live to father the children they should have fathered, to do the good things they should have done in life.

For generations people have prayed in gratitude: our nation is sound and unseparated. It was held together by the courage of people like Elon Farnsworth and those who died with him, and those who died in hundreds of other battles. The great crime never came before, it never followed afterward: the sadness of Americans meeting Americans in a death struggle, to wet their country's earth with the precious juice of their bodies.

Rock Creek ran bubbling behind hills where the battered Federal army hovered. Here, sheltered by fortified ridges, dirty canvas covers flapped in the breeze of evening; the straw was brought in armloads from stacks nearby.

The wounded lay weak and shivering. It was hot; it was July. The bodies of unhurt men were still drenched with sweat; but a dreadful chill creeps over the frame of a man whose blood has drained away. There were not enough surgeons, not enough stretcher-bearers, not enough bandages, not enough food. Dragging their sickly way through trampled fields, past the smoking craters which the enemy shells had dug, hurt soldiers went crawling into the woods along Rock Creek.

There was no more attempt to dislodge the Federals from their position. Lee had lost too heavily; his ammunition was low. He was far from home, with his fine army hammered to a pulp. There was nothing for him to do but retreat. Still the unhurt Unionists waited along the crest of those ridges, expecting at any moment to receive the orders from General Meade which would send them in counterattack against the Confederate troops.

The orders never came. Meade seemed to fear that his own remaining forces did not have the numbers or the strength.

Meade's headquarters were in a small farmhouse close behind the Union center, and staff officers' horses were tethered outside. Dead horses they were now—their poor twisted necks straining against halters which fastened them to the splintered fence. They began to bloat in the dusk . . . their torn bodies, their pitiful, large dead eyes seemed to accuse all men for this cruelty.

Weak lanterns glowed through darkness in hastily made hospitals by the creek. Surgeons did their best; they tied cords and rags around maimed arms and legs, seeking to stop the flow of blood. They had buckets; they brought water from the stream to those who were wailing for it.

At last some wagons containing food were driven near, and soldiers worked through black hours with the mutter of thunder coming close. They used their bayonets; they ripped wooden covers off boxes of crackers and passed these dry, crumbly bits to the wounded, clustered everywhere along that valley.

The thunder was not an empty threat; the

lightning did not flicker in vain. Shortly after midnight the skies opened. Rain fell in a mass, and soon the cringing thousands, behind or between the two armies, were drenched through and through. They lay in mud, in spongy pools of water. Rain hammered the darkness.

Thus it had happened after other battles, immediately after other artillery duels. It was the hand and act of God, many believed: the Almighty was punishing survivors for the hatefulness they had wrought. Others, trying to explain the crashing storm by more scientific means, insisted that the shudder of the cannon themselves had upset the clouds, the currents of air far above. The cannon made the rain fall with violence, they believed, as it would not have fallen otherwise.

Whatever the reason for the storm, it was smashing the shredded countryside, the shredded men who lay unprotected. The plight of those along Rock Creek was worst of all. Soon the stream, fed by fresh rills from higher country along its course, switched at the very crest of its banks. Soon it spread, filling flatter portions of the valley, sweeping angrily through thickets, among trees and roots, rolling the wounded men along in its tide.

There were screams. . . . "Help me. For God's sake, save me! I'm drowning!" Soldiers went dancing crazily through the torrent, grasping at the wounded, trying to tug them to higher ground. The word went back to positions on the ridge. Other troops came stampeding, some led by their officers, some breaking away without orders to go to the rescue of their friends. Still, many drowned who needed not to die, who wished not to die.

When Rock Creek went back into its banks at last, people walked in daylight and saw a hideous mat spread over the lowlands on either side: rags, clothing, weapons, knapsacks, the sodden mass of soggy crackers, and poor mute bodies wadded through the whole.

All day on Saturday, July 4, the two armies faced each other silently. They lay like crippled animals, licking their wounds, and more rain came pouring through the afternoon. Thunder boomed as if it were the cannon of the Lord, celebrating in queer and awful fashion the day of independence, the day of the country's birth.

There would be no more battling at Gettysburg. Lee had begun to gather up his wounded on Friday night—those who lay within his lines and close at hand. A train of wagons many miles long was filled with pale soldiers, young men with straw in their hair, mud on their faces, stiff, ugly bandages chafing their flesh. The wagons were guarded by General John Imboden's cavalry as they started their trek southwest toward the

Potomac. The whole Rebel army, the crumpled and defeated divisions still able to carry their muskets and haul their cannon, followed on through Sunday, July 5.

Meade's army pursued, but with much caution. Bands of blue cavalry hung snarling on the flanks of the Secesh retreat. In one town a mob of citizens rushed into the road when the Confederate horsemen had passed. They began to chop at the spokes of wagon wheels. They cut the harness and tugs of teams; they broke the wagon tongues. These wagons had to be abandoned, but the bulk of the defeated invaders moved on through storm and heat, pressing toward the Potomac.

The river was flooded when they reached it. The Confederates turned and stood at bay, holding off the Yankee hordes behind them. But during darkest hours the river began to go down. It was shallow enough for the divisions to proceed; so they crossed, beaten and hungry, but safe again within the borders of Virginia.

A tired staff officer rode up to General Lee. "They're all over, sir. They're all across the river."

Lee whispered, "Thank God."

——— 10 ———

THE HURT AND THE TIRED

Lee had been forced to abandon many of his soldiers; they had fallen too near the Yankee lines, they could not be recovered. Back in Gettysburg and the surrounding countryside, soldiers went toiling through sticky pastures and barnyards. They carried stretchers; they hunted for more wounded; they found them by the thousands. Every clump of gooseberry bushes gave up its quota. Some could be helped, even after this long horror of rain and neglect. Many were beyond all help.

The hot sun made the fields steam on Monday and Tuesday. There was a stench you could almost see as the Federal soldiers went about their hideous task of hunting the wounded and burying the dead.

Every large building in the village became a hospital: churches, lodge halls, many private houses. There were practically no ambulances. The wounded had to be carried in hay carts, and all who could even hobble were obliged to walk, seeking whatever aid the tired surgeons could offer. Once again roads were crowded with traffic—the traffic of mercy this time: doctors, nurses, volunteers, they hastened to Gettysburg. They came from Baltimore, Philadelphia, Harrisburg, New York, a hundred other towns.

Organizations which had been so helpful before this in the North—the Christian Commission and the Sanitary Commission—found a new and mighty task. Tents began to flap in the valley of Rock Creek below Culp's Hill, and along the York Pike east of town, near the end of the torn-up railroad.

Only a month before, it had been suggested to General Halleck, the Union Chief of Staff, that the Federal army adopt a system like that of the French. In France an ambulance brigade went along with each separate unit of the army. Halleck regarded this as a foolish notion. It was unwise, he announced pompously, to try new things like this. Then came Gettysburg.

In churches the pews were pushed together face to face to form great troughs. Here the wounded lay: cooing and wailing, dying in delirium, dying silently . . . only another face to be covered up with a soiled sheet, another motionless form to be removed.

Shovels of the gravediggers thudded through mornings and afternoons and on into the evenings, as long as men could see to work. Black laborers were imported; some of them were freemen, others runaway slaves. They toiled as they had never worked before. There were no bulldozers, no steam or electric scoops to make ditches: the shovels dug and dug. It seemed like trying to dip up the ocean with a sieve.

Another invasion occurred, and this time there was the sound of wings instead of spades. Buzzards: the ugly creatures whose only food is carrion—the hooked-beaked birds which subsist on dead flesh.

There had not been any buzzards dwelling in the woods around Gettysburg for a long time until this year of 1863. Then, strangely, a few weeks before the battle, people saw buzzards. It seemed now that these first birds had been scouts, warned by mysterious means and sent ahead to examine the country. However it was, they came back, and more came with them, and more and more. . . .

One day not too many years ago, the author of this book climbed the hill of Round Top and wandered into the woods on the easterly side. He heard a harsh cry, a movement of heavy bodies. He looked up. Buzzards—a flock of them. They lived in a rookery; the ground beneath was white with their droppings. What could so many carͻn lovers find to eat in a neat, tidy farmland, when it had been generations since the fields were plastered with horrid shapes of the dead?

No one could tell. The buzzards did not speak. They rustled uneasily on their perches, gazing out across the wide valley where the host of monuments stands.

More than seven thousand soldiers were killed at Gettysburg. There appear to have been about thirty thousand wounded—some authorities say many more than that. Records were badly kept, and no wonder. The bulk of the Union army was trailing along on the heels of the Confederates as they retreated toward Virginia. So many of the officers and adjutants were left lying at Gettysburg that the details of disaster were never kept properly.

Then one must consider that in those days men had their arms or legs amputated when nowadays it would not be necessary at all. Today these men would have penicillin, sulpha drugs, and always antiseptic dressings and instruments, to say nothing of x-ray apparatus, plastic surgery, and the other merciful gifts which modern years have brought. But, in the Civil War, arms and legs were sawed off by the thousands, and the destruction did not stop with that. Nearly a third of all the amputation cases died afterward. It seems that not seven thousand but more than ten thousand men must have died at Gettysburg or immediately following.

There were no trained medical corpsmen: only a few surgeons—no regularly enlisted nurses. Bands of brave women labored along with both armies throughout the conflict. Many of them went from place to place, following troops, climbing among grieving heaps on the battlefields at night, trying to help.

North and South, these were merely patriotic volunteers—middle-aged people, many of them, who had sons or other relatives gone away to the fighting—who wanted to do what they could. These women put on their shabby calico gowns, wrapped themselves in shawls, tied their bonnets into place, and went to war with a pocket Testament in one hand and a pot of tea in the other.

The famous author Louisa May Alcott, whose books *Little Women*, *Little Men*, and *Under the Lilacs* have delighted young people for generations—she served her stint as a volunteer nurse. So did Dorothea Dix, Clara Barton, Walt Whitman the poet, Mary A. Livermore, and hundreds more, with equal devotion.

People such as these swarmed to Gettysburg, but still there were scarcely enough hands. Church groups, lodge groups, Ladies' Aids—they came to spread the straw on the floors of hospital tents, to wall the open spaces on the sides with boxes, to wash the hot faces, to stir great kettles of soup.

Each house or building where the wounded lay was marked by a red banner. These thin red flags drifted lazily in the summer wind above throngs of people who pressed along the narrow brick sidewalks, many of them come to search for relatives who might be needing them. In the roadways men squatted atop wagons loaded with white stuff: chloride of lime to spread over the putrid ground, to try to stamp out the odor and seeds of death.

Our world has not gone very far in learning how to prevent war, but at least we have learned to prevent much of the misery caused by war. Can you believe it?—Organizations of trained helpers, bent on taking care of sufferers, have been in existence for only about one hundred years. Through all the centuries before that, men clashed against each other and then marched away, leaving those who could not travel behind.

If a soldier was too badly torn to be able to limp along on crutches or with his arm in a sling, he had to take his chances alone. Sometimes kind people who lived nearby would give shelter to the pitiful boys who crept to the doors of their cottages, but only a few could benefit from this.

It was Florence Nightingale, an Englishwoman

with a great heart, who changed all that. She went to the Crimean battlefields in southwestern Russia during the wars of the 1850s and thus became the founder of the charities which we now know as organized and businesslike assistance to an army.

If a soldier fighting for the United States nowadays received the sort of neglect which most boys received in earlier times, his family and friends would be writing to Congress. There would be columns in the newspapers, angry voices on the radio, a national scandal.

In 1863 the care of the Gettysburg wounded fell on whatever volunteers—private citizens, fathers, mothers, aunts, sometimes young boy and girl cousins—could make their way to Gettysburg. And no one thought it odd. These people spent their own money for carfare, brought their own lunches on the trains or in carryalls, and expected no pay or benefit from the government. They wished only to do whatever kindness they could for the helpless soldiers.

In town after town lamps burned in churches and city halls. People worked into the nights, packing boxes to ship. Everyone brought what he or she could bring from home; some could afford to bring very little. Everybody was trying to help.

Home-canned jars of fruit, applesauce, beans, big sacks of rusk (a kind of toast), jellies, lengths of flannel, old dressing gowns and slippers, books for the wounded to read. Little bottles of cologne. The common household medicines of the period: spirits of camphor, turpentine. Boxes of talcum powder, plugs of tobacco for those who smoked; forever and ever the masses of lint (cotton cloth scraped with a knife to form a soft loose fuzz used for dressing wounds, instead of the efficient slabs of gauze we have today). All these things and a thousand other items found their way into boxes and barrels.

Some would be addressed to certain groups: the Harrisburg Christian Commission, the Baltimore Methodist Ladies' Aid Society, organizations already in the field. Others would have but one word painted on the lids: GETTYSBURG. Boxes and barrels came heaped high in freight cars. The railroad had been destroyed close to the town. All the trains had to stop two or three miles short of the city.

Many stories have been told about the reaction of people in Gettysburg and the surrounding region. There are tales of families who fed strangers cheerfully without pay, day after day, until all the flour was gone—all their salted beef, all the green things out of their gardens. There were families who let exhausted strangers fill every bed in the house, and themselves slept on the floor or on a porch. This was something they could give: shelter. They wanted to help.

There were stories, too, of mean-faced farmers

who jogged back and forth from railroad to town and hospital tents in their wagons. The wagons were filled on the outward journey, empty coming back. Often in that day a wage of one dollar per day was considered ample for a working man. (Meals sold for five, ten, or fifteen cents apiece. You could dine on luxurious fare in many towns for a quarter.) But certain cruel farmers charged the wounded men three or four dollars . . . there were stories of men paying ten dollars merely to be hauled that short distance to the railroad track.

The word had gone around: trains would run to Baltimore and Harrisburg. All the wounded who could manage to drag themselves to the railroad would be carried off to bigger and better hospitals in other cities. Eventually they might recover enough to go home, or to rejoin their comrades in the army.

Boys staggered along. A stronger man would have his arm around a weaker one. A soldier with a swollen foot would sit by the roadside trying to whittle a rude crutch out of a tree branch. Here was one, crawling on his hands and knees, his trouser legs worn through by the stones, bleeding at the knees and elbows. Then he sprawled motionless. Others staggered past him. The word would go ahead eventually: *Dead man back here. Better have someone get him.*

Waiting on the railroad were "ambulance

cars." These were merely old-fashioned freight cars filled with straw, and with their ends knocked out, so that men lying on the straw could have the benefit of fresh air. In these cars the soldiers could be hauled away free of charge. But no means had been set up for transporting them to this haven.

A farmer's cart rattled on the road. Two or three wan-faced soldiers, wearing bloody bandages, sat weakly on the floor of the cart. A cry came from the roadside; a hand was waved. The farmer stopped his horses.

"Hey, listen, mister—take me to the railroad?"

"*Ja.* You got five dollars?"

"No, mister. I ain't got but eleven cents in currency, but I'll give you my mother's name. You can write to her; I know she'll send you five dollars—"

"*Nein,*" and the wagon would rattle off, the wounded man left by the roadside. It is an old truth that warfare brings out the very best and the very worst in human beings.

Wise people had foreseen that some sort of hospitals would have to be provided at the end or beginning of the active railway line. Within the first days after the battle, great tents were set up in this spot. There were only two trains a day, and often the tired men would creep into the little camp to learn that the last train had gone. Except for the thoughtfulness of people who had prepared the hospital camp, there would have been no food or shelter for any of these unfortunates until the next day.

The government gave its help: it detailed a throng of men who had been working on the railroad, and soon these big fellows were helping in every way they could. They spread clean straw; they brought blankets to cover the shivering. They set fires to roaring in old sheet-metal field stoves.

They helped to make panada—also known as ponada, ponado, or panoda. It was common invalid food during the Civil War, when there were few luxuries, soft and nutritious, which frail suffering people could eat. It was often made in buckets under the direction of the busy women of the Ladies' Aid. The buckets had to be cleaned carefully. Then they were filled with dried rusk— a kind of toast. Then a few spoonfuls of melted butter were added along with half a bottle of brandy and some sugar. Sometimes people were lucky enough to have nutmeg for flavoring. In the end boiling water would be poured over the whole mess—sometimes, if they were lucky, hot milk.

Panada may have tasted something like milk toast. It does not sound too pleasant. People who grow persnickety about their carefully selected lunches today should imagine what it would be like to be faced with a tin cup of panada. But there were better things sometimes: broth made from veal and vegetables, big bowls of cornmeal mush. It was an age when people did the best they could with what they had.

And the whole gruesome business would continue long. The bulk of disordered, smelly field hospitals would be emptied of their burden by kindness of death or the ambulance cars before the end of August. But many men could not be moved so soon. They lay on the cots or pallets to which they had been taken first.

Bit by bit, the smaller temporary hospitals in private homes or in tents were broken up, and the wounded were collected in a larger, more permanent structure called Camp Letterman on the hills east of town. (This camp was named after the chief surgeon of the Federal army.) Through weeks which followed, Camp Letterman was able to move its burden away. This had to be, for winter was coming; the wounded could not live in those tents through colder months.

The last miserable trainload was hauled off behind a noisy little locomotive on November 17. That was on a Tuesday. Wednesday, the eighteenth, a tall, shambling man would ride up from Washington. He planned to make a little talk at the new government cemetery on Thursday afternoon.

138

11

A DAY IN NOVEMBER

Mrs. Klappen and her neighbor across Middle Street, Mrs. Fliegerbach, put on the hoops they rarely wore; they put on their best once-turned gowns over the hoops. They scrubbed their children's faces, wiped smudges off the tight-buttoned shoes, and took their children by the hand. They went along with fifteen or twenty thousand other people to the speech making.

It would be, folks declared, a splendid speech indeed. *Ja*—he was a great man—so handsome, so silver-haired, so impressive. He was more impressive, they believed, than Grandpa Gernstaber, who lived with his niece around the corner from their homes. Grandpa Gernstaber could read books filled with Latin words; and not even writing were those queer marks of Greek that he could read also!

But this speaker who would talk today had been an ambassador. He had been also a minister, secretary of state, president of Harvard; and he was said to be the greatest orator since Daniel Webster. It was wonderful to think of the fine address which Mr. Edward Everett would utter and the brilliance of his appearance!

Also the President of the United States would be present and would say a few words.

The President was not happy on this Thursday, November 19, 1863. To begin with, he was a worried father. His youngest surviving child, Tad, was sick as a cat. The doctors didn't know what ailed the little scamp—hadn't known, at least, when Mr. Lincoln left Washington. Bob was away at college, and his mother was fit to be tied. Willie had died less than two years before . . . now this illness of Tad's. . . .

Some people, invited belatedly to put in an official appearance at a ceremony like this, might have backed out. President Abraham Lincoln didn't think that he should back out.

He tried to forget his spoiled, gabbling child. He tried to banish the vision of a hot, fever-dried face, and the hand wringing of the noisy woman who would be hovering over Tad's bed at the White House.

This trip up here to Pennsylvania was important—it seemed so to the President, anyway. People had told a lot of yarns about him when he visited the battlefield of Antietam previously. They weren't very pleasant yarns. The stories related that Mr. Lincoln had joked in public, that he had recited vulgar rhymes while passing the graves of soldiers who had died in Maryland to uphold his dream of national unity.

Well, the stories weren't true—not as printed in the newspapers. But folks had been bitter in their reaction. Abraham Lincoln was going to have to show them that he could behave with reverence and dignity in the dedication of a military cemetery.

Abe Lincoln had worked on his speech before he left Washington. Short, short, short—and to the point—that was the way he planned it.

Folks explained about the graves, the new cemetery, when Lincoln took dinner at Mr. David Wills's house in Gettysburg on Wednesday night. All the Union dead came from northeastern states—states which began with Minnesota and nudged each other all the way to Maine and Maryland. The identified dead would be buried, according to their regiments, in a great semicircle.

As purchasing agent for Pennsylvania, Mr. Wills bought about seventeen acres on a hilltop where some of the worst fighting had occurred.

Bodies had to be lugged from all over. They were dug out of the clefts at Little Round Top. They were lifted from clay of the railroad cut at Oak Ridge, from battered wheat fields and orchards in between. They were scratched up from near Sherfy's pigpen, and from behind Mr. Codori's barn.

Nobody as yet had been able to do much about the rotting horses and mules. Carcasses were all over the place, polluting the autumn air. Farmers felt that they had quite enough to do to repair their walls, to prop up torn fruit trees and put shingles over the gaping holes in their roofs, without wasting time on the wholesale cremation of horses. They wanted the government to pay for this damage.

The President's sad, angular face might well twist wryly as he thought of it. Some of these farmers were demanding payment because dead youths from Connecticut and Wisconsin had lain flat in their vegetable gardens, and had the earth dumped over them, right where they died.

It would be a great speech, a wonderful speech, delivered by the Honorable Edward Everett. But where indeed was the speaker? Mrs. Fliegerbach and Mrs. Klappen and their neighbors, and all the popeyed, restless children stood pressed in the crowd on that newly disturbed hillside near Ever Green cemetery. Mr. Everett was late.

Bands kept playing, to while away the time. It had been a remarkable procession, with soldiers and sailors in uniform, governors, firemen, mayors, Masons and Odd Fellows and Knights Templar and Knights of Columbus; and, of course, the President.

He was so homely. *Ach*, it gave you a pain. He looked like a cartoon in a city newspaper: high black hat, black suit, long pantaloons. His horse was too small for him. And people who stood close and heard Mr. Lincoln speak to his companions said that he had a shrill, high voice, and talked through his nose. That was no way for a President to talk.

But it had been a fine procession—down Baltimore Street to the Emmitsburg Road, and then branching off on the Taneytown Road. And the other throngs crowding along the sidewalks, and strangers in buggies. Country folks were standing up in their wagons. Little boys climbed high in the trees to see above the crowd.

The President squeezed two sheets of folded paper within his pocket; he put his gaunt hand in to make sure the paper was there. He had toiled over this speech—if you could call it a speech—for hours the night before, revising, adding, taking things out. Yes, he had chewed it like an old hound working on a dry bone. He hoped it wouldn't sound bone-dry.

Let's see. That beginning . . .

The Baltimore band was tuning up again.

Hail, ye heroes, heav'n-born band
Who fought and bled in Freedom's cause. . . .
And when the storm of war was gone
Enjoyed the peace your valor won.

The President sat pinching the unpressed cloth drawn over his thin knee, trying to fit remembered words to the boom of instruments. "Enjoyed the peace your valor won." Well, some thousands of warriors hereabouts would be enjoying only the peace of beetles and rotting acorns and good Pennsylvania dirt.

The dead weren't all moved yet—only a few of them. Mr. Wills said that the digging, the moving, the reburials had been in progress for only about three weeks. Now the coming of frost would put an end to such work until the frost got out of the ground next spring. Mr. Wills said that they figured there were about a thousand Unknown—maybe more.

"The peace your valor won." Maybe peace would come in time.

And the speech . . . let's see . . . how had he started it, to begin with?

It was over eighty years since the nation found birth. Lincoln first planned his speech as beginning, "Eighty-seven years since, our fathers brought forth—" That wasn't very smooth. "Four score" sounded better than "eighty." More dignified. Dignity was important on this day. "Four score and seven years since—" No—"ago." "Ago" was better still.

Lincoln dreamed back. Eighty-seven years ago ... there were men in powdered wigs, crowded arguing in that Philadelphia hall only a hundred miles away, sticking their necks fairly into the hangman's noose as they signed the Declaration.

A long time, a very long time. Thirty-three years before he, Abe Lincoln, was born—a whole third of a century before he was born. He was going on fifty-five now. He wondered how long he would live. To be eighty-seven—to be four score and seven himself? He guessed not.

Lincoln felt a shudder between his shoulder blades. It was kind of chilly up there on that platform. The President wished that he had a shawl. Would the perils of the present be understood in a distant future? Could he describe them to an age that felt them not? Who, he thought, would even remember that he had lifted his voice at Gettysburg?

Some said that Mr. Everett spoke for one hour and fifty-seven minutes. Some said that it was well over two hours from the time he began until the moment he reached his final words: "Down to the latest period of recorded time, in the glorious annals of our common country, there will be no brighter page than that which relates the battles of Gettysburg!"

Everett seemed to think that folks would remember; and Lincoln knew that he, himself, was prophesying it.

He had something to say about that recollection—at least that prophecy of recollection—among his own brief remarks.

The leading orator of the country had just finished a noble speech. But the President felt no real jealousy. He knew that he could accomplish nothing stately in the oratorical line—full of fuss and fury, quotations from the Greeks, and five-legged words. Lincoln knew that whenever he started quoting folks he usually ended up by quoting some old bumpkin he had known in Sangamon County, Illinois.

Abe Lincoln knew how his voice sounded: it was always high-pitched—especially when he first began to speak. It was a mannerism which he couldn't seem to shake off, no matter how hard he tried.

Who were those folks singing now? Oh, yes, a glee club from Baltimore, someone had said; and B. B. French had composed the very ode they sang. Too bad that Longfellow, Bryant, Whittier,

Lowell, or some other popular poet hadn't been able to produce an epic or a dirge for the occasion. They had been requested to try, but apparently they were all too busy. Chances were that it didn't seem an important enough affair. Just some more ceremonies over another pile of dead bones.

Of course, this was unusual: the bones were up in Pennsylvania this time—not down in Maryland or Virginia or Tennessee.

His friend Ward Lamon introduced "The President of the United States," and Lincoln got up and moved forward, drawing the precious folded papers from his pocket as he went. There was a certain amount of applause and commotion. He wondered whether there would be any cheers after he had finished.

He hoped that the newspapers wouldn't be too hard on him. But probably they would be. Probably it was a good thing for his peace of mind that he couldn't see just how some of the papers would react to this.

Take the New York *Tribune,* for instance. They would introduce his effort with one line: "The dedicatory remarks were then delivered by the President." The Chicago *Times* would be worse—speaking of his "ignorant rudeness" and "silly, flat and dishwatery utterances."

The London *Times* would jeer through the

mouth of its American correspondent: "The ceremony was rendered ludicrous by some of the sallies of that poor President Lincoln."

Perhaps worst of all would be in what amounted to the local press: the *Patriot and Union*, published in the Pennsylvania capital. "We pass over the silly remarks of the President . . . we are willing that the veil of oblivion shall be dropped over them and that they shall no more be repeated or thought of."

Wind moved along the hilltop and carried the scent of dead horses still bulking in the ditches where they had been dragged. Wind gathered up a taint of other decaying meat.

People coughed, people whispered, children ran on the outskirts of the crowd, boys went scrambling heedlessly among fence rails, hunting for relics. Kez Watson had just found a broken bayonet, and Bije Offendocker had a cartridge pouch with the flap torn off.

With more politeness, the crowds gathered nearer the speakers' stand tried to pay heed to the tall rusty figure on the wooden platform before them. Mrs. Klappen and Mrs. Fliegerbach gripped Johnny and Sarah and Freddy by their hands and held them in restraint.

Ja—he talked in a high thin voice . . . what was he saying? They could not hear him well.

Mrs. Klappen and Mrs. Fliegerbach had half

their minds concerned with the suppers they would need to prepare before Papa and Louis got home that night. There was the baking to be done the next morning, for a church bazaar too. Sugar doughnuts—glazed sugar. Always they sold well. The last time Mrs. Klappen had cooked and sold five dozen already.

They tried to listen.

No one might make them understand what the nation was like four score and seven years before, or what it would be like four score and seven years in the future.

No one hallooed, informing them that they were listening to the most famous words of the American tradition, spoken here for the first time.

Lincoln's Gettysburg Address

Four score and seven years ago our fathers brought forth on this continent, a new nation, conceived in Liberty, and dedicated to the proposition that all men are created equal.

Now we are engaged in a great civil war, testing whether that nation, or any nation so conceived and so dedicated, can long endure. We are met on a great battle-field of that war. We have come to dedicate a portion of that field, as a final resting place for those who here gave their lives that that nation might live. It is altogether fitting and proper that we should do this.

But, in a larger sense, we can not dedicate—we can not consecrate—we can not hallow—this ground. The brave men, living and dead, who struggled here, have consecrated it, far above our poor power to add or detract. The world will little note, nor long remember what we say here, but it can never forget what they did here. It is for us the living, rather, to be dedicated here to the unfinished work which they who fought here have thus far so nobly advanced. It is rather for us to be here dedicated to the great task remaining before us—that from these honored dead we take increased devotion to that cause for which they gave the last full measure of devotion—that we here highly resolve that these dead shall not have died in vain—that this nation, under God, shall have a new birth of freedom—and that government of the people, by the people, for the people, shall not perish from the earth.